What **Coffee** Taught Me About **Love**

"Served cold, hot and everywhere in between"

Ruth V. Frierson

Edited by: ViviStone (fiverr.com/vivistone)

Artwork by: @Dtayart

ISBN: 978-1-737005322

Dedication

This book is dedicated to my village of love. To those that cared enough to teach me love and have walked along side me despite the peaks and valleys. To my spouse: Amor, thank you for teaching me that love is more than a feeling, and when handled with care, it can bring more healing than any hurt or trauma, including mine. Thank you for being the platform from where I soar. As we are closer to the end than the beginning, I want you to know that I would do it all again if it is with you.

To my best friend, Lisa; sister, thank you for the laughter, tears, unconditional loyalty and committed friendship. There is no one like you and no one like us. You are the reason I savor every moment in life.

To my squad 3 x 2 x 1; Asylyr, Jess, Carinne Carinne and MXG. My life and love are incomplete without you. Each of you inspires me to be a better version of myself. To my many nieces and nephews who have shared some of their time with me, you have enhanced my life's journey.

Col. Colburn, KG, PTD, K-San, and SM, thank you for seeing my potential and changing the trajectory of my life.

Thank you for elevating love.

CONTENTS

Introduction

All that we learned and heard about love, we had to unlearn. This is a journey of that painful, but necessary and useful process. Like many, we minimized loved to a series of transactions driven by pride and confused as love. We traveled on the "me train" only to learn that that path was a lie. Fifty-fifty is not enough to sustain love, and if you are counting or, in any way, tracking, that is also not love but a business transaction disguised as love. We learned that the thrill of new cannot and does not sustain love. In fact, seeking a new thrill can and does destroy the path to long-lasting love. We've learned that love cannot be hidden; if it must remain in the dark, the shadow cast on it will eventually make it lose its luster.

Love, as we learned through trials, tests, tribulations, and triumphs, is much more than a feeling; deeper than knowledge and stronger than determination—it's the enemy of pride. Love grows uncontrollably deeper and more authentic; the more you give it, not the more you expect it. My love for another is not dependent on what the other does for me but on what I do for the other. It defies logic, but it lives in its truest and purest form when it is given without expectation. In our story, it did not take two to break it or to make it; it took one.

Through our story, I learned to appreciate the words of a wise old woman who answered the question that is usually asked of those with many seasons of marriage behind them; "to what do you attribute your 62 years of marriage?" She warned before giving her answer, "You will not like my answer because it is not what you would define as a romantic answer". The interviewer proceeded to encourage her to answer the question anyway. She answered, "We weren't always in-love, but when I was out of love, he loved us enough for the both of us, and when he was out of love, I loved us enough for both of us." We were young and in love when this interview played on television. Little did we know then that this wise woman would be speaking life into our own marriage.

Our story is one of deep hurts, offenses, disrespect, separations, and circumstances that neither of us ever imagined enduring, much less surviving or fighting to keep. This is a story of unconventional love, the love you don't look for and the one you want to leave but can't live without. We died a hundred deaths along this journey of ours so that the entity of us and all that is before us would not only survive but thrive.

With death, the dying of our painful past, selfish pride, and the healing of trauma came rebirth and second and third chances. We took a chance, sometimes we lost, and sometimes we won, but every time that we dared to lose the 'I', the journey led us closer to 'us'. Today, I can't understand how I love you more than yesterday, but I know it is mercy and grace that will have me love you more tomorrow than today. Today, I don't know how many tomorrows we have ahead of us, but I know that for as many or as few as they will be, they will not be enough.

There is nothing about this painful journey that I would change. I hope, I pray, that women, wives, and partners who have had to be strong and independent find the trauma that robbed them of their ability to live a full and vulnerable life—a life of courage, not fear disguised as strength. I hope couples that have managed to make an irreparable mess of their marriage find hope to persevere and turn their mess into a masterpiece, not seeking perfection but the revelation of self and a renewal of love.

Apart from me you can do nothing.

John 15:5

1

Devastation

I walk in, exhausted from the many things that can go wrong in one day. One day? I think to myself and chuckle quietly. I wish for those days, the days when the exhaustion was from the burdens of one day. In those days, my body could recover with a good night's rest or a long warm bath with some smooth jazz playing in the background and a glass of wine within my reach. This, however, is more than a day or even weeks, more than months or a year; this is a season, an almost five-year season. In this season, I lost my best friend of twenty-six years to the different types of cancers that ravaged her body. Each type too aggressive, even for a courageous fighter like herself. Her opponent was too apathetic to the love she had for her children and grandchild, the love that fueled her strength to withstand every pricking, prodding, surgery, and medical intervention so that she could have a chance to live. This intruder was too belligerent to listen to my pleas and negotiations with the Almighty for her full recovery.

I've lost my authority, influence, and status at my job practically overnight after twelve years with the same company. One change in management and poof, I go from being awarded a hero's medal to being viewed as a threat. For all intents and purposes, I've lost my lifelong, fun-loving and risk-taking confidant as he goes through a messy divorce. My health is in question, with debilitating pain in my lower back that runs down my legs and makes them feel weak. Walking, moving or sitting without pain is impossible these days.

Each of these stages in this five-year season can only be described as the global warming of my life. Sometimes drought and sometimes floods, but both extreme and always guaranteed to leave behind loss and devastation. Always leaving the same question behind; do I leave and start over somewhere else far from the devastation, or do I stay? Is my determination enough to rebuild from the rubble? The problem with seasons of drought is that most times we don't know it is a drought until we are in it. Therefore, it catches you unprepared. Each day finds me asking, "How much longer will this last?" Will I survive it, or should I leave? The floods are sudden, and although we might get a little advance notice, we are never prepared for the devastation they leave behind in a relatively short period of time. Sometimes my season, this season, feels long, like a drought, and others fast, like rushing water taking with it everything in its path. Although nature plays a role, many times, extreme weather is caused by the conditions and actions of man. In this case, it was the condition of my heart. And much like the lack of rain that changes nutritious soil to dry land, so does a lack of love harden hearts.

My friend's first cancer diagnosis came, as most do, I suppose, unexpected, amid our plan to enjoy our lives together in our senior years. We talked and laughed as sisters do after a little bit too much wine and reminiscing on the ignorance of our youth. In our youth, we counted ourselves blessed to have married mature men. Our husbands are seven to fourteen years older than us, and we anticipated we would outlive our husbands and move in together in our old age. We would keep each other company, we thought, much like Clairee (Olympia Dukakis) and Ouiser (Shirley MacLaine), in one of my favorite movies, *Steel Magnolias*. Sometimes friendly and sometimes fussing, but always caring for each other. Little did either of us know then that our friendship would play out more like Bette Midler and Barbara Hershey in *Beaches*.

In this season, I find myself engaged in daily and intense negotiations with the Almighty. I list the things I will do and how he is to respond, and I lay out the path that will lead back to her health. As her health gets complicated, a stranger reaches out to me. First, she invites me to meet her for coffee and to talk. I not only decline her invitation, but I outright reject her invitation and rebuke her for thinking I need anything from her, much less friendship. I have no time for new people in my life and even less patience for strangers. I recall thinking that she clearly did not know me, I am not even a coffee drinker, and right now, my focus is supporting my friend on her journey back to health. Who has time to form new friendships at a time like this?

Lavandi's chemotherapy treatments continue and are not going well. Her medical team shares the news with her husband and with me that this cancerous intruder is not responding as the medical team had hoped. The stranger reaches out to me again. "I am calling you to see if you have time to get together for coffee?" she asks. I am not only surprised that she contacted me again after my previous rejection, but I am also intrigued by her persistence. But once again, I reject her offer. Who has time for socializing when my negotiations do not appear to be effective? I recognize that this level of urgency requires that I add sacrifice to my pleas and negotiations. This time I promise to give things up in return for what I most urgently desire in this moment, her health. I don't promise to give up all things at this juncture since a good negotiator, like myself, knows to withhold some things in case they can be leveraged later. I am proud of my skillful strategy. With this strategy, how can we lose this fight? Eight months later, the strategy works, and my friend is declared cancer free. Grateful for my skills, I quickly forget, or maybe I choose to leave behind all the promises I made in desperate haste.

As quickly as I forget, the intruder returns, and it returns with a vengeance, aggressive and in different forms. The second time around, it was on her other breast, and soon after, we are told a different type of intruder is in her ovaries; this intruder will have to take precedence and be removed by surgery. Almost as soon as they wheel her into recovery, they find the spot on her lungs. I notice the invisible but heavy weight on Lavandi's shoulders as she considers her treatment options. I conceal my disappointment, recognizing my limitations. I can be with her, but in these decisions, she is alone. The well-renowned research hospital and medical team provide their expertise, but the decision to opt for surgery is hers alone, to remove an intruder that appears to be moving much more aggressively around her collarbone. This medical team—a reason for hope—specialized doctors, a prestigious hospital, the best heavy-weight fighter, and the best negotiator, there was no way we would lose this battle. Cancer had never encountered a better and more determined team. This time I add promises and sacrifices to my negotiations and prepare for the ultimate victory on what has been a long and painful journey.

To escape the grim news, I turn to my confidant and lifelong friend and brother, Roger. Roger is four years my junior and can normally be counted on for a good laugh or a quick pick-me-up. I update him because, as my confidant and friend, he understood, without explanation, the love shared between Lavandi and me. I see the love, concern, and tenderness that has been constant and dependable since we were children. I also understand Roger's posture and the look in his eyes that wishes he could reach me and attempt to soothe my hurts, but his marriage is ending. As these endings usually go, many are the people hurting through this process. Many are the people that need tending, and many are the things competing for his attention. I recognize that this time he would have to give all of himself to healing some hurts more important than my own, his children, those I counted and loved as my own. Without a need for words, I understand and release him from my burdens. His needs were unquestionable, and I was committed to being there for him to help alleviate his burdens. I knew this role. It had been there my entire life, the role of the "fixer". More than a "fixer," I was the director in the lives of my parents, siblings, and friends. Counting myself the most resourceful among my ten siblings, even though I was eighth in line. I would gladly tell them what they needed to be doing, how, and when. I was such a fixer that when the family came to me with their issues, big and small, I would often complain, forgetting that I had allowed and sometimes created this dependency that I now grumbled about. Now, I needed a shoulder, and the shoulders I usually leaned on were unavailable.

I turn to my work to soothe all that ails me and to be my confidence booster. Certain that the genius—that is me—will find the solace I seek in my achievements. I swiftly discovered that work can fill my time and even occupy my mind, but it cannot change seasons. Declared a public health hero just a few months before, but a change in management quickly dissipated my survival strategy. The more I worked to prove that I was worthy of respect and trust, the things I value most, the more repressive things got. I remember sitting in her office, across her desk, for the second or third time this week, when I realized what she was asking of me when she asked, "You know I have a doctorate degree? Are you aware of how you make everyone around you feel?" By the time I left her office, her message was crystal clear, know your place, or I will make you so uncomfortable that you will resign. She did just that for about two years, and I submitted my resignation, but not like she or I had anticipated or could have imagined.

My most faithful and lifelong companion, my pride, ever-present, silent but deadly, fed my ego, and my ego kept my pride in overdrive. Pride asks, so what if your best friend is sick, and your confidant is busy with his divorce, and your circumstances at work have changed, you still have jogging, right? Go for a jog and soothe your soul. I reply, in my mind, you are right. I can jog even longer when I'm stressed or upset. As I stand to walk up the stairs to change into my jogging gear, I fall to my knees and find myself with excruciating and unexplained pain in my back, right around my waistline and at the bottom of my spine. What is this? Is this a joke? I ask. It must be a joke; it must be! I attempt to move and shake it off because it is beyond unbelievable and, more importantly unacceptable, at this particular time in my life. I muster all my strength and will myself up the stairs but find that I can only crawl up the stairs on all fours, one painstaking stairstep at a time. I make it to bed and wonder in an irritated tone, what is happening right now? I protest to the universe and ask what do you want from me? In what can only be described as a distant but clear and loving voice, I hear my spirit answer, "I am here. Come, you can rest in me". My faithful companion, pride, quickly brushed this off and goes into a rant about my best friend's illness, my confidant's divorce, my work and influence, and my health. You've taken everything I rely on; now, whom do I turn to? Again, a clear answer, "Me, I am here." I respond, "I've called on you before, several times, and you have not answered, so why would I turn to you now?"

A cortisone injection in my spine brings some relief to the pain in my back but not to the pain that is to follow.

I walk in, and you are waiting for me. I see you, my husband but a stranger. I notice a look that has become familiar in the last two years but never this intense or poignant. Your mouth opens. I sense the anger that has now grown routine, but this time, I feel it. I begin to fear what it will be this time, what will come after I hear you say, “sit down, I need to talk to you”. You go on, “I’m going to talk to you; I don’t want you to say a word, just sit there and listen”, as you point to the furthest chair across the room. I feel your words and notice the anger on your face. A face I know well. A familiar face. I know every crease that forms when you smile. I know the brow that raises from one corner when you laugh. The way one side of your mustache is fuller than the other. The perfect proportion of your nose to your face. Why now, only now, do I notice just how unquestionably handsome you are? I’m lost in my thoughts of you. The man I’ve been with for over twenty years but only now do I see you. Why is it that I can only see all that is beautiful and great about you now? Where have I been that I didn’t acknowledge your strength and the gifts you brought before me daily? As your words cut my spirit like lashes on the skin, I wonder, not if I’ve lost you, but have you lost yourself? I’ve never seen this side of you. I’ve never seen wrath in you. Did I bring this out in you, or did she? And as the question in your voice brings me back to the present, the anger in your eyes transports me to a place unfamiliar to me. Your voice demands an answer. “Did you hear me?" "Yes, I heard you," I respond. It sounds like I am in a tunnel; the echoes are not loud but ring sharply and repeatedly in my ears. "We have come to the end of our journey together. I am no longer in love with you, and I don't think I ever really was", you say.

My health, my friend, my job, and my confidant—a season of drought, but this can best be described as a flood.

Every ending has a beginning. Now that I sit across from you, but further than we've ever been, I listen to you as you end our marriage. I remember the way you would recount the story of our beginning, when love had not been tested and when the season was fresh, and all things from the rich soil flourished beautifully. Unbeknown to me, you had seen me from a distance but could not get to me and then set out to search for me. On the day you saw me, you knew that I had just moved to the area, and people would have noticed the new resident. Just as you had given up hope on finding me, we ran past each other on a staircase. There I was, running down the stairs while you ran up the same staircase. Your search was over, you would recount. I was leaving from visiting a friend as you were on your way to visit one. Other than visiting friends, we had no reason to be in that building, on that staircase at the same time, and thousands of miles from our respective homes. You quickly notice that I ran past you without a second look, without turning back around to notice you, or without so much as a pause or a sign of curiosity. I ran past you without noticing you. This was not something a tall, dark, handsome, talented, and popular ball player was used to. You turned around and followed me out the door and into the street. You caught up to me and introduced yourself. We exchanged information. You said you'd come visit me later that evening, and I agreed.

I don't remember if you visited me that evening, but our first date was on the 4th of July, and I had moved there in mid-June. We were in Europe, and you and a friend of yours, Todd, picked me up and we drove the winding roads of a lush countryside that led us to a beautiful lake. I don't recall if the friend was your idea to make me feel comfortable in a faraway land or if that was my request, but I was glad he joined us. I immediately appreciated Todd's presence, his laugh, and his company. He easily joined our conversation but also knew when to excuse himself so that we could engage in deeper conversation and begin to get acquainted. I appreciated you for making me feel comfortable in this new environment and with you, a stranger at the time. We selected a spot and laid out our picnic blanket and drinks. I, in my socks and shoes, with a layered shirt and jean shorts, was clearly overdressed for the occasion at this semi-nudist lake. You had apparently been here before, I thought. You were comfortable and confident in this space and suitably dressed for this scene. I certainly should have known better. After all, it was Europe. I was uncomfortable at first. Unsure of where to land my eyes that would be deemed appropriate and comfortable. I quickly noticed that I was the only one uncomfortable; people of all sizes and every age, from children to seniors, were enjoying themselves with little care or concern for who was there. Families were enjoying their surroundings and the weather. They would change out of their wet bottoms into dry clothes. Nudity did not appear to be tied to morality, beauty, size, or even sexual connotation. Just families enjoying life and the summer weather, all in its natural state, place, and people included. People with their picnic baskets and children running around enjoying the warmth of the sun and the relief that cool water brings on a hot day.

You and I talked for hours and laughed often, and dusk seemed to come too soon. I don't remember much more about our first date, but that evening in my bed, I remember feeling an ease and a comfort that was new for me. I recognize now that it was your confidence and the swagger of a city boy that helped me be confident in myself and in those moments shared with you.

Early in our courtship, I was forthcoming and shared with you that I was in a relationship. A relationship I was trying to end but was not over. My partner at the time was insistent that the relationship could be saved and convinced himself that he could make me happy in life.

He promised more than I wanted or had interest in. Little did he know then that marriage was not an allure for me, and had I given it much thought or consideration, it would probably fall more in the category of a nightmare. Marriage was not a dream, a wish, or a desire I had. There was nothing tempting about falling under a man's rule or dominion. The more he insisted, the more he showed up unannounced, and the more the guilt for ending it subsided. He, with his words, insistence, and promises, was making it easier for me to disconnect. I often wonder if men or women are aware that the more you hold on, the tighter the grip the more suffocating it feels, and the easier it is to disconnect. Who wants to volunteer to be responsible for someone else's happiness? That is too much pressure and way too much power for any person to have over another. You, at the time shared that you were not in a relationship. I would quickly come to learn that not being in a relationship did not mean the same as being alone.

The invitation to your basketball games, where you were the guard and clearly the star of a very talented team, provided a crash course into your life. I was introduced to your world, your life, and your talents. I was provided with a peek into your popularity. You were popular among sports enthusiasts, women, especially among women, from people with influence and power to those who occasionally enjoyed the sport, counted themselves among your fans.

I don't know if that was the intent of the invitation, but unlike you, I was not gifted with an athlete's coordination, skill, or even understanding. Maybe that explains my lack of interest in sports. You, however, took the time to fold me into your world. You introduced me to sports, basketball and football, especially. You were teaching me to understand basketball and as a result, it exponentially increased my appreciation of your talents. As time went on and I became a part of the crowds of fans and joined you behind the bench, I grew to be an avid and loud fan of the sport and of you. I understood I was one fan among many. Countless were the women that would come near the bench to hand over their phone number, their notes, and other things. I was not always certain what was among those things left for you, and I did not ask. I can't recall if I was not that invested at the time or if it simply did not matter because I was secure in what was loosely—us. I don't ever remember asking, and I certainly don't remember you providing an explanation. Maybe it was that we both understood that these were the things that came with popularity, or maybe you made connections with some of them that I did not know anything about. Either way, you and I were close and together almost every hour of the day that was not taken with work or practice, but we were not yet exclusive. Things moved fast; three months after our first date, you asked if I would consider moving in together. My quick answer was no. Today, I still believe that, in that moment, you believed my answer was based on my moral values and that those values informed my decision to not live with a man unless married. This is what I believe prompted your next question, "Will you marry me?"

Many are the plans in a person's heart, but it is the Lord's purpose that prevails.
Proverbs 19:21

We rejoice in our sufferings, knowing that suffering produces endurance, and endurance produces character, and character produces hope, and hope does not put us to shame.
Romans 5:3-5

2

Promising and Plans

One month after we were engaged, you flew home to the city you were born and grew up in. Family and friends eagerly waited for you to join them in celebration of your friend's union to his longtime love. A community that was familiar with your past but knew little to nothing of your present. I secretly hoped you would reconnect with your live-in girlfriend from your home city. I had read her letters to you. The ones you kept in your top drawer. I had seen her picture. A tall woman, with a beautiful and flawless complexion, in a leotard, popular at the time, clearly an aerobics instructor or the like. She was not the only one. There were lots of letters in that drawer—notes of expressed affection and admiration from across the miles and from across the street. Hers, however, conveyed more depth and vulnerability, as if formed from fear or experiences of pain over the loss of love or connection. She loved you deeply; I thought to myself, certainly more than I did at the time or ever thought I could. At the same time, I thought it was wrong for anyone to love someone more than themselves, as her words detailed and clearly expressed. The other letters, words or notes of affection fell short of her devotion, her wishes for your prompt return, and her deep desire to try again. I felt her loss and hoped, for her sake, that on your trip home, you could salvage that which you once shared. I thought of you back at your hometown, enjoying all that was familiar to you, surroundings, friendships, family, and good times, and I was certain you would return and cancel our engagement. Saying you realized, in going home, that you moved hastily in your proposal, saying you wanted to try again with that beautiful woman from your hometown.

I was surprised to see you return unexpectedly soon from your trip. You were standing there with that smile, waiting for me after work. You were happy to see me, happy to be back. You looked like you belonged more here than there. This was now home. As you filled me on your visit, I surmised there was no rekindled love connection back at the city of your birth. Yes, no longer a hometown, but a visit to the place that birthed you, a place that was a witness to your past, but today, as you shared your story, you owned this space, this time, and confidently claimed your journey. You were confident, in us, in you, and in our future. You were hopeful, and it was contagious, but was it real? That same day I went through your "love drawer" to look for mementos of your past before I came into your life, to see if you had added to your letters, looking for any signs of a rekindled love connection. I found and empty drawer. Every letter, note of affection, and token of admiration, including all pictures, were gone. It was as if you had gone home to make peace with your past and decided to live in the present.

Is this love? Is this what love looks like? Giddy, full of hope, joy, excitement, wonder, and faith in the unknowns of tomorrow? I was not sure. I decided that if this was love and it made you happy, I would let myself be loved. I enjoyed the hopefulness that your presence brought to my spirit and my space. It was more than I had ever experienced for myself or around anyone else. Your light was so bright that it cast no shadow on who I was and where I was in my journey. The way you cared for me, tender in the way you held me, attentive with your words, and engaging in your conversation. Eager to share your music and your space. The ways you stood tall when you held my hand and drew me near to you. Your embrace not only drew me to your chest but closer to your heart. I remember the strength of your hands and the security of your embrace—security I did not know I needed.

A few days after your return, we were at my place, relaxing. We suddenly heard an unexpected knock at the door. A gentleman from somewhere in my past, but that I could not specifically place. I was not necessarily surprised since you were popular, and he began speaking to you as soon as you answered the door. I figured it was a fan of yours. In my curiosity in trying to place him in my memories, I stood there and observed the interaction, and then I saw you wave me to the door. I approached, and you asked, "Do you know this man?" Not sure of the meaning of your question, I reluctantly said "yes", still seeking to place him in my memories. And then the exchange came rushing back to me. We had taken a course together, and the best I could remember, we had engaged in a spirited debate. I think we had lunch or dinner once with some of our classmates. Why was he here, at my place, and looking for you? At my place. I was wondering how he knew he could find you here at this time. And then I hear your next question, "are you engaged to him?" I am so confused, and right now, I'm not certain what is happening and why you are asking such a ridiculous question. "What?" I ask. I can detect that you are not joking, and you are visibly upset. I see your mouth move, but your words sound warped. "This guy says you are engaged to him and that you are going to be married", you say. I repeat, with what must have been a dumbfounded look on my face, "what?" I look at him as if looking for an explanation that would make sense and simultaneously wondering if this experience was real. You repeat your question, louder this time, "Are you engaged to him? Do you plan to marry him?" I respond more decisively this time, "no," I say, "why would I marry him?" You repeated, "He says you are going to marry him". Again, I look over at him and ask, "What gave you that idea?" He says, "I've watched you every day; remember our argument?" Argument? What argument? He must be referring to the debate; it was a spirited debate, which is what makes it memorable, somewhat. It was a debate in a classroom setting, sir, as I go through the memories in my mind. He continues, "remember when we ate together, I love you, and I will make you happy; he won't. He sees other women, you know?" I still cannot wrap my head around what is happening, so I go through a list in my mind, what could I have done to give this man this idea. I direct my questions at him; "Have we been on a date? Have we kissed? Held hands? Anything? Did you ask me to marry you?" Because if we did or you have, I have some bad news for you, those interactions were not memorable at all. So many thoughts and questions are racing through my mind. Then his answer comes, "no, but I love you". Sir, you don't know me, is what I want to say, but this scenario is so unbelievable to the point of ridiculous. Then I hear you interject, "man, you need to get out of here", and before I can put my thoughts into words, this situation gets much more ridiculous with his next words directed to you. "Okay, I know you think yourself a great ball player, so I will play you for her". What? Did I hear this correctly? I am standing right here, sir, and I am not a prize to be won. I mean - I am, but who I marry will not be decided in a ball game. Then I look over at you, more for confirmation of what I just thought I heard, than for an answer, and realize you heard the same thing I just heard. "Maaaan, are you crazy?" You repeat yourself, more sternly this time, "Man, you better get out of here!" He walks out, and you look at me, visibly upset, but why with me, I wonder. I can't explain what just happened myself. All these years later, I still can't. Days, weeks, and months after that bizarre encounter, it seemed that he would know every time I would be alone, as if he was stalking me. He would suddenly show up where I was and when I was alone, always alone, always trying to make "friendly" conversation. As I started to worry for my safety, just like it started, it abruptly stopped. I was relieved but also angry. Angry I had not spoken up for myself. Angry, I had not told him what both he and I knew; he did not love me or even like me; he couldn't have because he did not know me. He was obsessed with needing to possess that which his boy ego told him he was entitled to have, simply because he wanted it. Just like the men I've known all my life, with nothing to offer but feel entitled to have or possess simply because they want. I wish I had had the time and courage to unleash my thoughts and tongue to slash that fragile boyish ego. I knew I had it in me, but once again, when I needed my voice, it grew silent.

As our relationship continued, the whispers about you intensified. We see him at this club, we see him at that club, and we see him accompanied by women, always. Women of every hue, height, and culture were the reports from those I knew and those I didn't know from your foes as well as those you would have considered friends. I was not phased. Maybe I should have been bothered by it; maybe I should have brought it to your attention. Maybe I should have joined you to places where you invited me to be at your side. I had no interest in the places you frequented or your activities. I was not worried. I was content involved in my own things and enjoying my own space and mini-explorations and adventures. I had always been comfortable enjoying my own company and saw no problem with you engaging in the things that you enjoyed doing. I was busy making new friends in this new place, far from all that I knew. I was happy to be away from all that was familiar to me. I socialized with people who introduced me to new activities, dancing to new and different music, dining on new foods, and even engaging in Taekwondo. As an introvert, socializing could be exhausting, but I made sure I took time to recover and take the space to care for myself. I traveled with groups of people to different parts of Europe and really relished my freedom. I was enthralled by new places and intrigued by new opportunities. I enjoyed my time alone, my time with new friends, and my time with you. I never questioned if the rumor mill was true. I wonder, now, if I had inquired, would you have denied or confirmed if any of the rumors swirling around and about you were true. So, what if they were? I thought. I was happy for you, and I was happy for me. This arrangement, hardly a customary engagement, was working for you and for me. You, always a social butterfly, easily liked, and comfortable in rooms with small or large crowds. You eased in and eased out of social settings with confidence and grace. You were popular, people lavished on you, and you seemed to take it all in and enjoy it all. I admired all you were and how secure you were in how you loved and lavished on me. We knew who we were, together and apart, we cared deeply for each other, but neither needed the other. I enjoyed not having the pressures of being responsible for your happiness. Why would I want to change that?

I recall now, in this season of loss, a poignant evening in our courtship. One of my friends was adamant about having me join her for an evening out at a particular club. Maybe she knew you would be there since the club scene was her regular escape. She frequented clubs as much as you did and knew where the crowds would gather and on what days of the week. At the end of that evening, my group of friends and your group of friends ended up in the same club. We noticed each other from across the room, but we did not interfere with our separate gatherings. Once again, I took notice of your comfort and confidence in being the center of conversation and attention—clearly in your element. Everyone around you is attentive and enthralled by your conversation and demeanor. Just as you noticed me admiring you, I was asked to dance at just the right song, *Push It* by Salt-N-Pepa. My roommate had taken time to teach me some of her smooth moves for this particular song, and for just this moment, my moment to shine. I got on the dance floor confident and ready to display my moves, just as I had practiced them for days, for this one song. Less than a minute into the song, I feel a tap on the shoulder. You find my face, and I notice yours, no smile, and no laughter. The laughter that had just been on your face a few minutes earlier among your friends. You mouth some words that I can't make out through the booming music and the noise of people having a great time on the dance floor. You motion with your hand and your words are now clear "let's go". "I'm dancing," I say as if you had not noticed my perfectly choreographed moves. Of course, you knew I was dancing, but my instinct was to protect this moment that I had practiced and prepared for, for the last few days. I had to see it through. You obviously took it as defiance. Your next move, not one I had practiced or prepared for, is your hand on my sweater, dragging me off the dance floor. I was in disbelief since I had never seen this side of you. You demand we head home. I am embarrassed by the scene and walk away from you. I hear your voice loud behind me, "if you walk away from me now, it is over". I leave the club and you in my rearview mirror.

A day or two later, I was informed by my roommate that you had returned to the club to continue your evening of fun with friends. She has regrets for me, stating I should have stayed. I assure her I am comfortable with my decision, but she doesn't hear me. I am attentive and begin to understand that she is projecting and promoting her agenda. She does not believe or is willing to accept that, at this point, it truly does not matter to me. It certainly does not matter to me as much as it matters to her. I take note of her excessive investment and take steps to build boundaries between us, choosing not to ignore her but choosing to protect my peace. What she does not know and what I choose not to explain is that on that evening, we had called off our engagement as I walked out and away from you.

Walking home that night in the dark and cold, I heard the footsteps of someone running behind me. I stopped and quickly turned around, relieved to find a friendly face. He placed his jacket over my shoulders, and walked me home in silence—understanding in the dark and without words I was not prepared to engage in conversation. I was not hurt, but my ego was bruised, my moment stolen, I was furious. Before we knew it, we could see the sun rising, and he invited me to breakfast. We had spent the cool night under the stars, eventually starting up a conversation that had lasted until dawn. He was sweet, he was kind, thoughtful, and a friend when I needed one. As time went on and our friendship grew, he asked for more, and I considered the offer, but it was not him I rejected. I just wanted freedom. I wanted to be free to do what I wanted, when I wanted, with whomever I wanted, without having to consider anyone or anything else besides me.

I had a plan and freedom. My plans excluded all the judgment and labels placed on a young lady like me. I would not worry or concern myself with the virtues placed on women by promiscuous men. I would not allow myself to be subjected to a man and would not be controlled by one. I would continue to carve my own path and decide my own fate. I would spend how and on what I wanted and would invest as I needed. Society would not place their morality on me like a burden or scarlet letter. I had learned, at an early age, not to place any value on what others thought of me. I was defiant as a young woman, and now I was free to live in defiance. I was excited about my future. A future where I exercised my own will and depended only on my own strength, leaving no space for vulnerability, disappointment or pain.

The freedom I envisioned was brief. You showed up at my place as if nothing had happened and we were moving on. It was obvious that this is what you were used to, but that would not be with me, I thought. I wanted no part of you or us, not because of the encounter we had, but because being free is what I wanted. Sooner rather than later, I relented. You promised things I did not ask for or care anything about. You said you would stop going to the clubs, and I assured you it was not necessary, not for me. You enjoyed yourself in that space and among crowds, and dimming your light was not something I required. Soon you were back to meeting the demands of your life of popularity and socializing, and I started cocooning at your place. I waited for you for whenever you returned from your travels or outings. Sometimes you would find me asleep, and other times, I was awake and eager to see you. We would slide into each other's embrace and find comfort in each other's arms and the warmth of our bodies. You thrived in crowds and enjoyed the attention, and I found solitude invigorating. It became a familiar and comfortable routine, you out meeting the demands of your popularity, me waiting at your place. I was there so often that I started to build a friendship with your roommate and his partner. They were gracious, including me in their conversations and their games, inviting me to join them for a drink or a meal. It started to feel more like a home and less like I was intruding into this space. Time went on, and your kindness, care, and attention for me grew. We cultivated a relationship that honored our differences.

One Friday evening, during your off-season from basketball, your routine was interrupted and ultimately broken. You passed by my place to pick me up, as had grown customary between us, and take me to your place. You were sharp, well dressed and well groomed, for your nightly outings, on schedule, Thursday through Sunday. Except for this time when you arrived, you found me sharply dressed, make-up and hair done, with heels on. I noticed the surprise on your face and detected the question on your mind. Maybe you thought I would finally join you. Before you could ask, I shared my plans and informed you I had been invited out by some friends, and I would be joining them this evening. I explained that I did not know what time I would return and not to expect me at your place tonight. I would see you the next day. You must have noticed my determination, and you turned and walked out. As you walked away, you requested that I stop by your place on my way out. I arrived, as agreed, and I was surprised to find you in bed under the covers. You explained that you had fallen ill unexpectedly. "I'm not sure what was wrong, but I think it is best if you stay and care for me", you said. I pointed out the obvious that you had just been fine an hour or so before. You insisted that you needed caring for and asked me to stay and provide the care you needed. I was young but not stupid. I heated up some soup, brought some tea to your bedside, and every type of medicine I could think of. But what medicine do you give a man with a sudden bout of awareness and regret and a case of manipulation? Certain you were fine; I went on with my plans for the evening. The next day you proposed we stop going to clubs unless we went together. I agreed.

Over the next few months, we would discuss the many reasons why our union would be challenging: our different cultures, customs, beliefs, and vastly different upbringings and experiences. Over the same few months, I would come up with every trick, excuse, and scheme to delay our nuptials. You, filled with promise; me, panicked with fears. We discussed children, daughters, of course, finances, the faith we would practice, and how we would establish a home. We understood the differences were wide and varied, and our experiences were distinct because of your city boy upbringing and swagger and my homegrown stubbornness being raised in the same state as Congresswoman Barbara Jordan. Pride and stubbornness are in the Texas soil that seeps into our blood. All that would have seemingly appeared too much and too vast to overcome seemed possible. No barrier too big to break through, no depth too deep to dig out of. Your confidence and hopefulness are infectious. We seemed aware and prepared for every eventual challenge, and with eyes wide open, we moved forward with planning our small wedding on foreign soil.

The things we didn't prepare for or chose to ignore were internal wounds. The wounds that from the outside we appear to have overcome, but from the inside have failed to properly heal. The wounds and traumas we ignored played a significant role in our raveling and unraveling. No matter how far we go from our place of birth, we take those wounds with us wherever we go.

We did what most young couples do with a horizon full of promise. You called your family and shared the news that you would be married. Providing details of who I was and where I was from. I stood by and listened and hoped for that excitement to be contagious, but it did not happen. I delayed sharing the news until a week before we were to be married. You noticed my hesitation and asked, “I think you are ashamed or embarrassed by me and who I am. Is that why you have not told your family?” I respond, “That is not it at all. We can call them today.” Of course, I was being honest. There was nothing to be ashamed about. What you did not know and what I did not share with you in that moment was that I found it unnecessary to share news of an event that would not happen. An event I knew I would find a way to sabotage. Most importantly, I did not seek, need, want, or value my parent’s approval or disapproval. You knew all there was to know about me, but in your own excitement, you wanted me to share the news, even with the people that I did not find worthy of including in my decisions. The moment I left home, or more accurately described, the moment they left me behind, their influence over my life ended, and I was all the better for it. I thought.

The day before we were to be married, on my bed lies open my personal journal. It contains my deepest thoughts, fears and reflections. It contains the dreams I share with no one. It is open to today's entry, November 2nd. I called you on the phone and asked you to stop by. I looked around; all was in place. Leaving no room for error or a way to be missed, I place a pen in between the pages. I looked out the window, and there you were; my heart raced, and I felt myself get weak. I think to myself; I can't back out now. It is now or never. I saw you approaching and prepared myself to walk out of my bedroom at the exact time that you walked in. Every second was planned out, all of it perfectly orchestrated. All that is left is to execute my plan. You walk into my bedroom with a smile on your face, and I quickly exit. "I have to go to the bathroom," I say, excusing myself. My journal entry should take no more than a minute to read.

Nov. 2

I am supposed to marry tomorrow. I am not a happy bride. I am nervous. No, I am afraid. I do not want to go through with this, but how do I tell him without hurting him?

Courage, I need courage.

I flush and wash my hands as planned. You will hear the water. Nothing can appear as orchestrated as it was. I walked in, and it worked! My journal in your hand and the look of devastation on your face that I had hoped for and expected. "What is this?" you demand. My response on cue was, "What? Why did you go through my personal journal?" I ask. You didn't flinch and said, "Tomorrow is the wedding, and it is too late to back out now. I love you and my best man, and I will come by to pick you up tomorrow. Be ready!" and you walked out. Wait! What? I saw the hurt on your face. You were supposed to dump me. You were supposed to cancel. I was counting on your pride to flare like mine does in moments like this. What just happened? It didn't work; it didn't work, I think, dejected. Except that it does. In this season, I am reminded that you are the best decision I never made. In this season, you loved me more than your pride. In this season, you loved me enough for both of us.

Love covers over a multitude of sins.
1 Peter 4:8

3

The Taste of Pride

The pride in me, the pride that has filled my head, my spirit, my soul, and has festered in my being for years—the pride that has been my security blanket. As long as I can remember, pride and I have been one. This pride that only my best friend would point out to me and describe as my worst enemy. I wondered how everyone else could have missed it or did they see it but dared not say it. Now I wonder if they dared not say, out of fear of my protest and retaliation or because they knew I would not or could not be convinced.

Now, as I sit across from you, my pride flares at the utterance of your words, "We have come to the end of our journey together. I am no longer in love with you, and I don't think I ever really was". I wish now that I would have listened then, five years into our marriage, to the sound counsel that came through the voice of my best friend Lavandi. "I tell you this because I love you, and nobody else will", she said during an eight-hour conversation, which sounded more like an intervention at the time, where she attempted to hold up a mirror to my pride. "Your husband loves you". I remember scoffing at her. "Listen, girl", she said sternly this time. "He loves you crazy. I see it in the way he cares for you, the way he looks at you, and in his expressions. He finds ways to serve you and anticipate your needs before you even put them into words." In my ignorance and pride, I respond, "Girl, he better. He knows I would accept nothing less." Her pauses always indicated the seriousness of our conversations and after one of those long pauses, she says, "Hey, what are you fighting? Whatever you are fighting you need to make peace with. You need to do that soon because if you continue, he might not leave you, but you will lose him." I, unflinching, never paused and therefore missed paying attention to the fact that it was not who I was, but who you were that allowed you to love and care for me like you did. How many times, things, moments, and opportunities have I missed to see you and appreciate you? To my shame, the answer my heart fears is far too many to mention. Your daily grind. Your battles at work where your expertise and knowledge are challenged by supervisors less qualified than you and staff questioning your leadership at every turn. The expectations placed you on by me, extended family and friends. I knew the burdens you carried daily and could only imagine the crosses you buried before you walked into our home. Yet as I look back over our lives, I am left to wonder and ask, and honestly, if I must ask, well then, I know the answer.

Did you ever find in me a healing hand for your wounds? Was I, for you, ever a place of rest? At the end of each day, did you find in my lips words of encouragement? Did I ever put forth an intentional effort to make our home a castle or a place where you found comfort? I know the answer to every one of those questions. That is what has me sitting across the room from you but miles apart. The more I hear your words, the more my spirit is crushed. Hope far from me, hate deep in your heart and anger unleashed. You repeat, "It's over for you and me, over, do you hear me?" Your eyes red, on your face - fury, where love, compassion, and happiness once lived. No signs left of that now; your words now swords that cut deeply. I see you, and there is nothing left of you now, nothing left of the man I once knew. My pride in position, my tongue being sharpened with every strike from your mouth and my ego pounding, saying, strike woman, strike! You know that you have it in you to seal this coffin. This relationship is dead, so bury him now. Once again, you speak, bringing me back to the present, a present that I prefer not to be in. You say, "Do you have nothing to say?" I take a deep breath. My pride wants to remind you of what you said when I first walked in; you said to say nothing remember, but most importantly, it wants to remind you of who I am. My tongue, the sharpest weapon in my arsenal of pride, is ready to unleash. Now is the time I've been waiting for; two hours of listening and I am ready. Instead, something unfamiliar or someone I don't know speaks. "I love you." You're fuming now, "What! What did you say?!" I take another deep breath, "I love you." Your words, poison to my soul. "I don't even like you. I don't like your cooking. I don't appreciate how you raise the girls. You don't keep a clean house". You go on. Every word a sting, not of me, but of you. I've had a sharp tongue over the years, but it is who I have been, never who you are. Even now, I don't believe these words in your mouth. I am sad, coming to the realization that I have done this to you, to us. I wish I could blame her, but no, she does not have that much power or influence; she is not that relevant. "Do you hear what I'm saying?" you ask. My spirit crushed; you think you have been victorious, and I am your injured opponent. The sad realization is that you have lost you. I respond, my pride wants to defend, but my response comes, "I hear you. It is over. You don't love me and never have. Is that right? Did I hear you correctly?" You look at me with the same anger of the last two hours, "yes that's right" you say. "So, what do you have to say?" you ask. "I have one request", I say looking at someone I do not know, "Can I give you a hug?" You look at me with surprise, anger just a little bit less evident, "What, why?" I see you defeated and exhausted from the burdens I placed on your back, and I say, "I just want to hug you". Before you can answer, I get up from my chair and walk across the room of shards and shreds, and I hug you. You don't hug me back, but your tears like a fountain flow, your sorrow deep, and you collapse into my arms. We embrace for a minute or two in silence, and then you pull away from me. I break the silence and ask, "Is that all you wanted to say to me?" Your reply, "Yes". I turn around and head out of the room, and before I walk completely out, your voice stops me. "Where are you going now?" "To our room," I say. "For what?" You ask. "To pray", my answer. Your voice once again stern, "Be done before I get up there". I offer to pray in a different room, and you direct me to stay in our room and pray. On this day, I engaged in the most intense battle of my life, not with you, my husband, but with my pride and the sharpest weapon in my arsenal, my tongue.

Before this moment, it had already been a tough season, a season of drought, where I had begun the journey of learning to die to myself. I had relented to that stranger's invitation about two years before and was intrigued not by her insistence to meet but by her resistance to back off or her lack of fear or lack of pride, never relenting to my rejections to her invitations for coffee. I do not know how she could have known that this conversation would come, but two weeks prior, she had warned me. Your husband will have a conversation with you that will be hard to hear. When it happens, listen not to what he is saying but to what he is not saying and pray before you speak. During your two-hour rant, I remembered her words, and this was the moment she said would come. I felt the anger from your mouth and recognized the unquestionable presence of negative vibes swirling in the air. It all felt heavy on my shoulders, suffocating, and I began to pray. By the time your onslaught of words was over, I was not expecting to have the opportunity to speak. Therefore, I was unprepared for a response, much less the response that came out of my lips. I, like you, must have been, was surprised. This is what it feels like to die to self, to reckless impulses, to the need to outsmart your opponent, to be the one vying for the last word, or the need to be right. Always winning the fight but losing my humanity. How many times had I exchanged the 'us' for the 'I'? Once again, too many to count. How many relationships end, and how much hurt do we inflict on one another in the name of protecting our pride? We pay high prices for cheap thrills. How many marriages last years and end because of a tough season? How does a man that once vowed to love me become my adversary? We were not coming to the end of our marriage, a marriage that started with so much promise and careful planning, because of finances, like most marriages that end in divorce. You did not lose your love for me because of our failure to communicate. That theory did not work in our favor. You communicated, often and clearly. "I need your respect. I need you to stop being disrespectful. Why are you so disrespectful?" you would say and ask repeatedly. I, unable to understand, ill-equipped for vulnerability, and not recognizing love, continued my path of needing to be strong, independent, and controlling. I heard but did not understand your requests, which to my pride, sounded like demands. Therefore, I was not equipped to respond.

It had been two years of you seeking solace somewhere else. You were seeking healing, understanding, respect, and your need to be seen. All that the popularity of being a gifted athlete had brought to you years before. That and the accomplishments of your career had been sufficient to maintain your confidence, despite my disrespect and lack of emotion towards you. Our daughters and my intentionality with them had been my drive; you and the way you cared for me had been my foundation and helping others, my reward, and the passion for my job fueled my purpose. All appeared to feed our needs and establish for us a comfortable life. Then, with time and age, the limelight brought on by your talents went away, and your career transitioned. My friends, career, and foundation were all simultaneously shaken. All that was left now was us. Except that us, without all those things and distractions, got lost. You, without the limelight, was back where you had started, needing to be seen and valued.

But now that I started to die to myself and I'm ready for renewal, now that I understand your language, now that I've learned the lessons, and understand the hurt and betrayal, now - it is too late for us.

You now choose pride as I choose you.

Pride goes before destruction, and a haughty spirit before a fall.
Proverbs 16:18

4

Stronger than Pride

It is a cold home I kept; I once heard a woman say in a movie. As rings formed in water after a rock is thrown in it, those words rang in my soul, small but repeated. A familiar reflex, my pride quickly assumed its protective position. It said vehemently, a resounding, no! Discard that from my spirit, far from my mind, and especially distant from my heart. Those words have nothing to do with me. Another sign, another whisper, from years ago, maybe even twelve years before this moment.

Years later, those words rang in my head, heart, and spirit, once again, as in a distant whisper, but still causing discomfort to my spirit. I was afraid to go back to them, but I forced myself. I watched the movie to test if I would feel what I had felt years before. Once again, it rang repeatedly in my spirit, but deeper this time. Once again, I ignored their call.

The punishment for failing or disappointing me is served in many creative ways; payback, revenge, intentional pain, moments of embarrassment, or withholding affection. Whatever the moment lent itself for. I was always prepared to serve it cold or hot, but always rich. Rich in creativity, strategy, and execution. If I felt slighted or shunned, it was certain, but not swift. I never responded with uncontrolled emotion but with careful and thoughtful strategy, considering what would be most adequate and cause the most damage. My cheap thrills became my protective positions. My weapon of choice always wicked, always ready to strike a blow—blows that cut the heart, the soul, and the spirit at the same time. Words with venom. The type that humiliates and suffocates, the type that leaves the opponent speechless. I was always proud of this quick-witted and wicked tongue.

Mouth almighty and tongue everlasting was how you would describe my mouth and I would pridefully claim it. I could and would deny you the pleasures of my company. I could see you and miss you and let you know it—intentional and long the coldness of my care. I laid eggshells everywhere in our home. Don't raise your voice, eggshell. Don't look at me that way, eggshell. Don't be late without calling, eggshell. Don't forget to kiss me, eggshell. Don't miss my calls, eggshell. Each time you stepped on an eggshell, the agony of my pain, the resentment of yours. Now I wonder how did you survive maneuvering through these eggshells?

Our marriage, like most marriages, survived eggshells, pride, separations, and betrayals. Throughout our marriage, there were many moments of joy, love, honor, elevation, and encouragement. There was much good we had built together—countless were people blessed by our union. We knew hurt and disappointment. I knew the hurt that I experienced from not having a voice, and therefore gave voice to others. You knew what not being seen or valued felt like, and that fueled how you poured into everyone around you.

Your ability to make friends out of complete strangers was a benefit to our family. You traveled for short periods, weeks at a time, and long periods that lasted a year, and sometimes longer. You knew you could depend on me to keep the family moving as you focused on your work. I was reliable and, as you described, honest, even if brutally honest. We enjoyed many moments of intimate laughter. The kind that only a husband and wife can understand. Together we formed our own entity. Ours was a strength that our families required, and we understood the pressures of meeting the needs of our extended family. We provided support for extended family in the form of monthly finances for our mothers, providing a home for our siblings, and rescuing siblings from circumstances that required our urgent attention. Family and friends knew that we would readily and gladly support and encourage those in need of our love and sacrifice. We came together to love, even if that love was outward-focused. Together, our entity – the one that needed to be heard and the one that needed to be seen, was kind, generous, thoughtful, and even sacrificial for others. We managed to see their needs and answer the call, not realizing the toll it was taking on us. Distracted from our own wounds, we failed to recognize our need to be healed. Not realizing that every rescue took us further from us. Caring for others became how we came together and a part of the way we lost our way. The more we gave, the more was expected, and the harder we had to work together to meet those demands. Working together built a strong bond between us, but that energy was for them, and we did not notice that we had less to give to each other. We failed to look internally. We failed to heal the wounds that festered, and we continued to strive past the hurts that were hurting us, but we did not see or acknowledge them.

We were that first-generation that made a comfortable living. Not wealthy by any means, but we did not struggle, and having more than enough to meet our needs, we could have things we wanted. We worked and enjoyed the work of our hands. We earned, gave with no strings attached, and recognized our position as a blessing that allowed us to share the blessings. As you often say, "we are only stewards," each time reminding ourselves not to rely on our finances for our happiness or security. Paying for people's meals as we exited a restaurant, paying for people's gas, groceries, or coffee, without them knowing, was our way of keeping ourselves accountable to not think of ourselves higher than we ought (Romans 12:3). In these moments we created a formidable entity. Our lives and upbringing as children are evident in the way we gave. We knew need, and we knew want, and our gratitude informed how and what we shared.

Our entity as parents, lucid. My dream was that my children would know no hunger or need, and they would know with all certainty that they were loved. Yours, the commitment to be present, involved, and loving. We were, for all intents and purposes, the parents we wished we had; for you, a present father and an engaged mother, and for me, the security and comfort of enjoying a childhood that did not have to carry the burdens of adulthood. We did not dwell there or delve into how our childhood was informing either of us. We only focused on providing a different life for our children. We understood that no other two people on this earth would experience the overwhelming joy we felt from hearing the laughter of our daughters as they played with each other as children or the laughter that comes from their teenage mischief. Who else could understand the pain that comes from their hurts? Who can understand our pride in watching these young girls become ladies and women in their own right? Each of them, different from the other with their unique gifts of inner beauty that radiate to their external humanity. In this, we were securely bonded and in agreement with our parenting. We certainly made mistakes, far from perfect, but we were thoughtful, intentional, and students to our daughters. We were constantly learning from them what they each needed. I remember my extended family's observation of them. "They are some special and lucky girls." It seemed like everyone in my family wanted to protect the world they lived in. You also, hearing from your family, and your response always the same, "those are my girls." They shared how, in your eyes, our daughters could do no wrong. You had made it clear where you drew a line of protection. In many ways, we lost our way, but our parenting was strong, secure, and loving.

The gifts I brought to our entity were valuable and efficient for your life. Your frequent and extensive travels required independence, flexibility, and an ability to continue life uninterrupted and with limited attention given to the disruptions that can come with frequent and long absences. My understanding of your role, position, and responsibilities ensured that you remained as worry-free as possible wherever in the world your work took you. My commitment to you was to do whatever it took to keep you focused on your task and to help ensure your safe return or, at minimum, ensure you excelled without concern wherever you were. Those long separations created bonds between us. When you were physically gone is when we created our closest bonds. We had to be intentional about using this time wisely and lovingly. In preparation for your departure, we painstakingly created budgets and plans for our separate lives. This ensured we could focus our phone calls and conversations on things that were fun and light. You talked to our daughters daily and to me at least twice a day. We used our talks to catch up on the mishaps in our lives—the unexpected snake in the grass as I was mowing the lawn, your well-used car, purchased for temporary transportation. It was meant to get you around, and sometimes it did, and sometimes it didn't. You would share how much you treasured the letters and pictures you received from our daughters. Sometimes their need of you hurt, but their updates and need for you always connected you to home. You, to this day, have every one of their letters, cards, and drawings, in your book of treasures. Distance, however, provides different experiences. Experiences that were uniquely yours and exclusively mine. We each had troubles to deal with on our own, and we did just that. We protected our limited time together to focus on us, our family and planning for your return. These physical separations from each other are the times we focused mostly on each other, and these created bonds between us. The bonds that sustained us once you returned, and we returned to our routine of focusing on others.

Your gifts to me were many. Your confidence was what a wounded child like me needed. It was not your job to heal my hurts, the wounds I did not see because they were disguised as strength and independence. But your confidence and love allowed you to withstand all my hurts that manifested themselves as strength but rooted in fear, seasoned with anger, and served cold. Your extrovert personality created a community of friends and a village of support for our children and for me. That village cared for us when you traveled. Your protection of us, always constant and reassuring.

Saturday mornings at 7:00 a.m. was the day of the week you and I would unwind and connect. We would go for our coffee. We'd always go to the same place, you'd grab your coffee, and I would grab my tea, and we'd ride wherever the road took us on our Saturday mornings. It became our relaxation and self-care routine. We would listen to our music—our music, the world's music. Our choice of music was influenced by our diverse hometowns, our travels, and the diverse cultures and customs of our friends that introduced us to many different genres of music, salsa, country, hip-hop, African, Tejano, jazz, and a variety of music from central and South America. Eventually, family and friends started joining us. We'd all grab our coffee and snacks, chat a little in the parking lot, and the caravan grew as more friends and family joined us. We had unintentionally started a tradition of togetherness. During these times, we would look for garage sales, bargains, antiques, etc. Every Saturday morning, a leisure drive of connection and creation of memories that now flood my mind. I wish we had that time back when doing nothing connected us more than anything we did and when hundreds and thousands of miles between us brought us closer together.

Our entity, as parents, thrived. Our entity, as givers, flourished. Financially secure. It seemed the more we gave, the more the Lord gave us. When we were physically separated, we made every effort to focus on connecting. We thrived when we served others. We provided a home for family and friends in need. Our home was the center of celebrations, outward love, and care for the wounded. Our reward was to see that those who had sought our support were now independently thriving. Our greatest joy was the laughter in our home from game nights or unexpected dance-offs, or our terrible attempts at singing.

Our love was best practiced on the wounded or those in need. Ours was a home for those that needed healing or hope; even as our unseen wounds festered, we were always ready to advocate for others.

But if anyone does not provide for his relatives, and especially for members of his household, he has denied the faith and is worse than an unbeliever.
1 Tim. 5:8

5

Emotionless

I remember our first indoor date, the one after the picnic at the lake. You set the mood. Kenny G. played the saxophone in the background, candles lit, dinner set perfectly, and you sharply dressed and ready for the evening. Although I remember it now, as my mind goes back to the beginning. It was always like that with you, attentive to every detail. I'm not sure if it was practice or if it was a space that you meticulously and intentionally created only for me, for us. I see it now, but I don't remember appreciating it then. Phyllis Hyman, Jeffrey Osborne, Stevie Wonder, Keith Washington, yes, a playlist that now plays back in my memory, but it had no value then. It is interesting that we get busy with the business of living life, but we don't recognize the moments we will, one day, treasure and remember most until they no longer are.

Maybe I never appreciated these moments because I found no point or purpose for them. The songs of loss or love. The rom-com movies. Funerals, yes, even funerals. "What is the point?" has always been my question.

They've always caused me to itch and almost retch. What is the purpose of feeling loss or pain? If I am honest, what is the purpose of feeling, much less feeling deeply? Where is its use? Where is the value? Why would anyone put themselves through these feelings? How is this a strategy for life? My mom had feelings, I remember, and they served her no purpose except pain and disappointment. I did not want to be like her.

If I had only laid down my pride or reflected on myself, who I was and why I was, I would have asked myself this question earlier; how does a person get here? Honestly, I had to have noticed something wrong, something missing in me, in order to pause and consider my best friend Lavandi's question, what or who are you fighting? I would have been open to the kindness and invitation of a stranger earlier. Maybe I would have found value in vulnerability or the peace that comes with surrender. Strategy was a reflex for me, and emotions did not fit as a useful strategy. This was my approach to life without further examination or thought.

Now, here I am, on my knees, weeping like never before as God continues to reveal me to me. In exhausted surrender, I still find the will not to fight but to beg; please don't let me remember.

I remember, yes, I remember, and I beg to escape the memory. I will not go there. There is where I have never allowed myself to go. The place I left and promised to leave behind forever, determined never to return. There is nowhere I want to go back to, but there is where my mind is taking me; a time when I was most vulnerable. A time when I had feelings and maybe the last time I did. There is where I learned to be motionless and, with time, emotionless. My heart races, my hands tremble, and my breathing is erratic as my brain drags my body where it does not want to go. Not there, please; that little girl in me cries out for help. My eyes push back the tears, but what about that lump in my throat and that elephant sitting on my chest. How do I dissipate the lump in my throat? Lord, please! I beg. Help me go forward without going back. I don't want to go back! I will be different; I promise to be better, to do better. Just please, Lord, don't let me go back there. I will tell myself to remember that I am strong. I am okay. I have overcome. Look at me, please. I have overcome! You know that I am resilient; I have been resilient, even purposeful. I serve children so that this won't happen to them. It proves that I'm fine. I'm fine. Please, no need to go back there. I hear my mother's voice, "Your father, before he died, said, maintained, repeated, and promised, that what he did to you was not that bad." She said more in the form of a question rather than fact. A question that she expected an answer for. Now an adult, I would not be manipulated. In my anger, I did not respond. I remember I left the room in disgust and refused her the answer that she sought, the answer that absolved her. I denied her, once again, as in past years, the absolution she was seeking.

Now I am here in this beautiful home but transported there, back to the room of my childhood, a six or seven-year-old lying-in bed, motionless, awakened from my sleep, wondering, what is this I feel? Only to awaken to a nightmare; who is this? What is happening right now? Praying a child's prayer; God, please let this not be happening. Whatever this is, don't let it happen. No answer. Another prayer, God, please put me back to sleep. No answer. Yet, another prayer, God, please let it stop. No answer. One more time, God, please save me. No answer. Yet again, God, please let me lie motionless. Thank you, God, for the many motionless nights.

I remember my father—tall, strong-willed, sometimes a tyrant, but always friendly and generous with his friends and extended family. As a child, I enjoyed playing with his thick ledger filled with blank checks, from which he paid his crew. Only an important man would have these things at his disposal, right? He would occasionally spend some leisure time with my brothers and take them fishing or teach them about the mechanics of cars. He would talk to my brothers about women, their purpose, and how they should be handled. My brothers were encouraged to exercise their prowess with young women. He was often disappointed in my oldest brother for not wanting to participate in this cat-

and-mouse game. He was proud to have sons and disappointed to have two daughters. "If she is a girl, you and your daughter can leave from there," is what my mother recalls him saying as she was in labor with me.

On his order, it became mine and my sisters' job to be taught to cook, clean, and press clothes at an early age. This was our training for what he envisioned our life would be. A life of servitude to our future husbands. In his eyes, there was no other role, purpose, or worth for women. My mother did as she was told, and we would get up early in the morning at 5:00 or 6:00 a.m. to start cooking, preparing breakfast, and packing lunches, under her close direction and supervision, for our six oldest brothers that worked in some capacity at the time. I grew to resent him, not for the 5:00 a.m. wakeups, but for the role he thought we would play in our lives as women. I resented him for the way he yielded his authority over my mother. I grew to hate him for the value of "worthlessness" he allocated to women.

His life as a narcissist distorted all that could have been counted as blessings in anyone else's life. A young woman who believed in his expressions of love only to find herself a mother of seven or eight at twenty years of age. Sons who admired him and would give their earnings to him every Friday so that he could then turn around and give them a small allowance from their own earnings. A home where he was received at any hour of the day or night with a hot home-cooked meal. A position of influence at his job despite his lack of or limited education. All blessings that he was not worthy of and that he never valued as such. His prideful "manhood" blinded his capacity to see anything or anyone as a blessing, much less grace and unwarranted favor.

My older brothers each left home as soon as they could. They would come back sporadically and momentarily, depending on their circumstances. Most of them, as young adult men, were old enough to leave but not necessarily prepared enough to survive independently. As a result, always finding themselves in need. My mother would always take them in and provide a roof over their head and a warm meal for them and the families they were now creating. My father would always take advantage of the opportunity to make a buck from their misery. Most of them, too caught-up in their own needs to notice anything amiss in our home.

My 2nd oldest brother, whom I looked up to and I was closest to, used to take me everywhere with him as a child, even on some of his dates. He was cool, kind, and attentive with me, but he married as a teen and moved out and far away from home to another state. My oldest brother had gone missing around Easter. A few days later, he was found in a grassy area near a river with tire marks across his face. This was the year I would be turning fifteen. I thought any of the two would be my mode of escape, as they were sometimes my mode of reprieve and, unbeknownst to them, my rescuers.

My oldest brother had planned an elaborate birthday bash for me; in just about six months, I would be turning fifteen. He would have turned twenty-seven the same month he was found murdered. He was the kindest and most thoughtful human being among us. His laugh was loud and contagious. His joy for life and his humanity for all people, but especially the most vulnerable, children and seniors—admirable. Truly an exceptional human being and the opposite of our father. I often wonder if he knew that his kindness was the reason our father did not like him. In our father's eyes, his kindness must have appeared weak. In his honor I went through with the party he had planned for me, but that evening I had to dance the traditional dance with my dad. He proudly strolled the dance floor with me, arm-in-arm, and then swung me around for my first dance. Disgust and disappointed in myself for not using my voice at that moment. I thought I would be sick. I was dancing with him as he stood tall and proud in front of all the guests. No one noticed my sadness, and no one noticed how sick I felt, how vulnerable I felt. No one noticed my internal shouts for help. I hated them all for watching this spectacle and not hearing my cries for help. I hated them for not rescuing me. Sick, I felt sick. Anger in the midst of celebration and sadness where happiness should have been. I finished the spectacle, chatted with my friends in attendance, and left my own party early. I would not and could not continue to lend myself to this. I recognized that evening that there would be no hero to rescue me, that no reprieve was coming. Every opportunity for escape gone, I knew somehow and someway I would escape the hell I was living in.

I was defiant as a teenager, but not as most teenagers are. I was strategic with my defiance, even and especially then. I defied all rules that placed a strain on me because I was a girl or a woman. I made home a battlefield. If I could not have calls from boys, I would make it a point to give out my number to boys I didn't even like and had no interest in talking to. Every time the phone rang, I made sure I would run to answer it, hoping it would be for my father or if I couldn't get calls, then no one could, except my mother, I thought. I would give boys my address to come by and visit, just like girls visited with my brothers. Most boys did not come to visit me, though, they knew I had many brothers, and none dared risk it. I was not worth the risk, and I hated their cowardness. Every move I made was defiant. I remember watching the *Young & the Restless,* and I was taken by Ashley Abbott. Ah! Yes! Yes! That is who I want to be like. Cunning, ruthless, strategic, comfortable in her skin, defiant, independent. Yes! One day I will leave this house, and that is whom I will become.

My father, with his drunkenness, had long ago lost his management position. His prestige and influence were lost as a result of showing up to work drunk one too many times. Now our family struggled to make ends meet. I, without a driver's license, would wake up early to drive my father's car to school, two blocks away, while he had to hitch a ride. I think he thought that if he ever complained, I would tell his dirty secret. I was not that strategic, but I was angry, angry enough to want to see him suffer in any and every way I could. I felt for my mother at times because she was caught in the crossfire, but I also disliked her for being weak in my eyes. Every day, I could feel my anger growing and my heart for others less present. Many were the ways in which I acted out my anger, but my lashing out was no longer enough. I remember the morning came when I knew this would be the day it would all end. Anger and defiance were no longer enough! It was a regular school morning; nothing eventful was happening this morning. No monumental markings that something within me was brewing. I just knew I was tired of feeling dirty. I was disgusted by his presence, his smile, his voice, and his breath. I had grown tired of not being able to bathe without knowing when he would walk in. I ran out of ideas on how to lock and block the door, all to no avail. Tired of not being able to be small enough to crawl out of that small window in the bathroom. Naked, vulnerable, humiliated, defeated, standing there with no escape. I would wonder, where did everyone go? Mom, where did you go? Sick to my stomach, tears in my eyes, and the scream for help stuck in my throat. I was frozen stiff in these moments, grateful for the water from the shower that mixed in with my tears. I would not show him hurt, but I know he could see shame. Shame kept me silent. I was always strategic, waiting for the right time to shower, the time when I knew people were around and they would notice if he walked in on me. I hated them all for walking away and leaving me with him or hated them for not noticing that he was missing out there and in here with me. I hated them for not asking where he disappeared to. Why would you leave him with me? Why did I have to be born a girl? Why did I have to be born weak? The humiliation of it all, to not be able to pretend to be asleep. Frozen, motionless, devastation to a child's soul, when you can no longer pretend to sleep, you are left to accept that this is not a nightmare you will wake up from; this is the reality of your life. He knew I was weak because he was my father, and I'm sure I once loved or admired him, and he preyed on my weakness. I am a child. I am a girl who hated her breast, and her womanhood, and I especially hated that I looked like my mom. He always said, "You look so much like your mom." "You remind me of your mom," he would remind me, as if excusing himself for his acts. God, why? Maybe if I didn't look like her and maybe if I didn't remind him of her, maybe then I would not feel him invade my body. Maybe then, Lord, I would not be disgusted with my body. Why, Lord, did you make me a woman? Why did you make me weak? Where is everybody?! Somebody, anybody, please help me! Who do I call on when the father that is meant to protect me is the invader, the rapist, the devil in the flesh?

I knew that morning I wanted to be able to sleep. I wanted rest. How long can I stop breathing and remain motionless, pretending to sleep? How long do I have to stand frozen? How many strategies can I develop to not be left alone in his presence? Many are the ways that he violated the trust of a daughter with her father. I had smelled the scent of selfishness, the scent of unadulterated power, and I was sick of it. It is a scent worse than liquor or cigarettes, worse than feces, it is a scent that is powerfully dizzying and sickening to this day.

I knew whom I could trust and whom I could tell. He had been caring, involved, and attentive, a leader that I looked up to. I ran all the way to school that morning as if escaping from something that was chasing me. He looked at me with kindness, not pity. That mattered to me then and has mattered to me since. He, with his compassion and not pity, made it okay for me to share my hurts. Things quickly spiraled out of my control. I got shuffled around, and my story repeated over and over in a day. It almost made me regret having to relive the memory multiple times in one day with different people.

I remember the humiliation I felt each time I was asked about dates, places, times, and how. The how, was the most traumatic to relive. I remember feeling like nothing more than a pitiful case that had to be processed and placed by 5:00 p.m., preferably. I don't remember compassion or caring, much less empathy. There were deadlines to meet, and efficiency was what mattered. I was a child, a teenage child, but still a child, and I did not understand caseloads and processes and 5:00 p.m. deadlines because people have their lives to live. So, the burden to ensure their process and efficiency was placed on me. Shuffled here, shuffled there, repeat this, alone in this office, then that office, alone, wondering what is happening—a doctor invading my body to confirm and invasion of my body. This process seemed cruel and cold. Expedient pity with zero empathy. Emotionless process. By that evening, they find a foster home to place me in. I arrive in time for dinner; a mother and two children, a boy and a girl younger than I, and a husband that they are waiting for so that the family could have dinner. I'm in a bedroom waiting. I hear the commotion of his arrival. They settle in for dinner, and I brace myself for the summons to join them. There was a quick knock on the door. I opened it and was handed (shoved, really, but I'm supposed to be grateful, so I'll choose handed), a plate of dinner. Shunned. After a busy day of shuffling around, being shunned is when I question, what did I do wrong? Is this woman upset with me because I did something wrong? Shame. I feel shame for reporting my father, inconveniencing my mother, and for this woman who is clearly upset that I interrupted her family and routine. Maybe she just feels threatened as a parent because I reported my own parent. My stay in this foster home was brief, too brief to come to an understanding of her frustration with me. I would see the inside of my bedroom and the bathroom. I would not interact with the kids or the family. I would not be allowed to leave the room except when I was picked up for school. But I suppose the caseworkers felt good for having pity on me, and the foster parent felt accomplished for providing a roof over my head. All in all, it seemed as though everyone felt good about themselves as I felt shame, shunned, and regret. I was returned home to my mother after my father was taken to jail. Unbeknown to me, this solidified that there is no purpose in feeling and strategy is important for efficiency. I learned I was a case to be processed, with as little emotion as possible, with a deadline to be met.

To this day, well-intended people of goodwill say, "You look so much like your mom", and that is when I feel emotion. My heart races, my skin crawls, and I feel sick and exposed, so much so that it makes me want to punch them right in their faces. And if I did, would they know it is my father who has robbed me of this being the compliment they meant for it to be?

For I will restore health to you, and I will heal your wounds, says the Lord.
Jeremiah 30:17

6

Meeting and Hating Esther

During the drought, while my best friend Lavandi was sick, before the flooding that came the day you informed me you stopped loving me, I was told about who she was. Although I had never seen her, I imagined her as beautiful as described. In my imagination, I could picture her always ready for his call. Preparing herself meticulously, attentive to her perfumes. His favorite, of course. Thinking of him and eagerly anticipating the moments she would see him. She prepared herself for him. I imagined her hair perfectly done, her skin glistening from her bath and perfumed oils, and her clothes carefully selected for these occasions. She lavished on him and served him with her body and beauty. She hung on to his every word. She made her bosom his home and her home his castle. There were no worries there; the cares were miles away. The wine was sweeter than ever, the music, festive, and the movements in her dance freeing and alluring to him. Free, I imagined, free from a wife of strife. Free from a nagging wife. Far away from the woman, he vowed to love forever, and his confidence grew. I wonder, was it her he loved or was it her ways with him? I see her in my daydreams, and she is the source of my nightmares. I imagine her captivating and enticing figure. It is said she is younger, always younger. I don't know for sure, but I know she is now the center of my prayers. Lord, why can't I be like her? But the truth is, I don't want to be like her. I want to be me, and that is why I'm sitting here, learning about her. How useless now, my pride. How useless my stings, so wise in my own eyes. Why did I place my confidence in my position as his wife?

Except that in my case, she is not like Esther. I don't know if she is beautiful or young, old, or my age. I don't know what she looks like. I don't give over to her, my time or my thoughts. She is not the focus of my nightmares - I am. I know that like a desperate and hungry spider, she weaves her web. She spins and weaves and polishes until it glistens. She grows her web because she is hungry. It is not my husband she weaves it for. She is just hungry for the next catch. She cannot occupy her thoughts with being selective because she is desperately hungry. The next catch in her web will have to be enough to satisfy her cravings. There is nothing new under the sun, and the trap is laid like it's always been, and like a confident but curious insect, he flies into it. Unaware of the entanglement because the web is new and shiny. Of course, this must have been built especially for me, he thinks. It is so enticing that he misses that it is a trap of lies and deceit. Her long legs and walk, careful but swift, her eyes wide and bright, her smile cunning, her hands eager, and as he becomes aware of her approach, she draws near. She wraps him tightly, ensnaring him in her cocoon. The more he moves in search of an exit, the tighter her grip. He is too wrapped up now to know that he is slowly losing air and altitude. All this time, he thought he was seeking freedom. As he was busy escaping and seeking to soar, he flew into a web, where he learned that all that glitter was not gold.

I remember the day the stranger and I met at Starbucks for coffee. She introduced me to Esther and to her diametric opposite, me. As the stranger had me read the book of Esther in the good book, the more I read, the more Esther made me nauseous. She was all I never wanted to be—her demeanor, her person, her servitude, all unfathomable and unobtainable. "Who are you in this story, Esther or Queen Vashti?" she asked. "I am the queen", my answer, not ashamed, but also no longer full of pride. I can relate to the queen, I thought, and there is nothing about Esther that is appealing. I then heard, "Esther is the goal," she said. "Are you kidding me? That is impossible!" I say in protest. She sips her coffee, and I think to myself, I've never liked coffee, and I don't like Esther, and now I don't like you; if Esther is the goal, I don't want to ride this train. However, what I did not like about Esther was what I liked about this stranger; she challenged me to grow. She reminded me of Lavandi in that way, never telling me what was easy to say or what was easy to hear—never letting me wallow in my hurts or suffering. Not letting me complain about my husband but saying, "take your eyes of your husband and put your eyes on God". Always with the good book in her hand. The stranger and I started meeting regularly over coffee. She asked, "What can you do to be more like Esther?" At this point, "Probably die and come back as someone else," I said, as we both chuckled. Over the next few months, dying is exactly what I did—dying slow, painful deaths. My ego fed my pride less often, and the more I starved my pride, the less sharp my tongue became and the more broken my heart got. Sometimes, I could feel myself choking from swallowing my words, probably from their bitter taste and sometimes from the venom.

Then the day came when she asked, "What if you served your husband as Esther serves her King?" I almost threw up just from the thought of that. "Nope!" I said.

One early Sunday morning, after the talk with my husband and months after I was introduced to Esther at Starbucks, I am strolling the isles as one does at Target (Tarjay). My cart was filled with purchases, and my husband was on the other side of the store. Unexpected tears roll down my face uncontrollably. Tears quickly turn into sobs. There, in the aisles of my favorite store, I'm crying like a kid who has been denied a toy. I cannot stop myself, though I try, and the harder I try, the more relentless my tears. I realize I'm exhausted, and my body now betrays me. I realize that this season has taken its toll, and not even my purchases at my favorite store can stop this torrential rain of tears.

I call the stranger. More as a reflex than an intentional thought or strategic move, as per my usual composure in every situation. I don't say much, but through my sobs I say, "I'm at Target." Her response, "I will be there shortly." Shortly was right, and I soon regretted it. It was the silence of our ride together that made me uncomfortable because in that silence, I cried like I had not cried since standing in that shower as a child all those years ago. She let me cry without asking questions or prodding. She hugged me with unearned love but without pity. Important to me. I was not worthy of her concern or her love, and yet there she was. We arrived at church service after about a forty-five-minute drive. I did not want to be there, but then I heard the pastor speak. He seemed to speak directly to me as if he knew I would be there and he knew my story. Once again, he was not saying what I wanted to hear, but his words were convicting. He spoke on love, not self-seeking, but sacrificial love. Christ-like, he said. Christ-like? I thought. What is Christ-like love? I knew of God, but not the Christ who laid down his life because of his love for me.

I remembered the person I had left at Target. The person I had vowed to love and who once loved me. Did we ever love each other with Christ-like love? As I was leaving the store in the company of this stranger, he had looked at me in tears, as if I was the stranger. I, in turn, looked back at him, wounded, lost, a stranger. I saw in his eyes, what he did not need to say, I want to reach you. I want to find my way back to you, but he couldn't, and he let me walk out of that store with no questions asked.

Next time I met with the stranger, who knew me more deeply than anyone by then. The one who had seen me cry and be vulnerable. I thought I would be embarrassed, but she did not give that a chance. She saw me, hugged me and had me read Proverbs 31 about the wife of noble character. What is this? Got it, I thought, granted I want no pity, but this! I don't want this either! How is it that you have me read this? This Proverbs 31 wife sounds like my mother, and that is the last person I want to be like. Ashley Abbott is the woman of my dreams. Is there anyone in the good book with Ashley Abbott's character? She is whom I want to be like and not this Proverbs 31 wife. Do you not see me wounded? Esther was enough, and now this! As we met more regularly, I then learned about the tongue and that it is better for a husband to live on the edge of a roof than with a nagging wife. Each time, each lesson, a stab to my pride. And then, the twist after the stab, she read, "be doers of the word and not just hearers." Wait, what?

These are not just stories that convict; I'm expected to live it. Then she read, "life and doctrine, let your life…" Enough! Enough! My ego was wounded, but not dead, "but he", I begin to protest, and she cuts me off. Take your eyes off him; she reads, "Remove the plank". "Oh, geez, woman, do you not see the hurt he is causing me? Do you not feel for me?" She answers, "of course I do, but what I feel and what I think does not matter. Only what Christ says matters. I love you too much to tell you what you want to hear. To let you talk badly about your husband. It is your heart, your sin, and He is calling you." She clearly notices I am upset, sitting there pouting, and then she says the last words I wanted to hear at that moment but needed to hear. "What do you think your husband, who has not left or moved out of your home, is seeking and FINDING in that woman? Do you think she lavishes on him, or is she nagging? Do you think she hangs on his every word or is her mouth constantly going? Is she praising him, comforting him?" She goes on. "What are you doing?" she asks, and my answer comes swiftly, "I'm hating Esther; that's what I'm doing".

I won't serve him like she does her king. I'm a good person, and good will have to be good enough. All I've been through in this season, and still, my pride thrives. It might be weaving and bobbing every time I listen or read a scripture, but dead it is not. What Esther does is listen, and her vulnerability is her strength and her humility her crown. That does not make sense to me. "Maybe in those times", I say. That is nothing more than a metaphor, my pride says. This, too, is not for you; my ego chimes in. That is right, I poise and gather myself. I'm a good person, and good is good enough. I rattle off the "goodness" of my ways. My pride reminds me of how lucky he is to have me. As I review those in my mind, my ego flares, and my confidence grows, but like a person falling from the sky, I am reaching but catching nothing, my arms flailing in the wind. None of what I'm seeking in my best is enough to save me from falling. As I fall, the scales in my eyes fall.

I see me. So good, so kind, in my own eyes. To the stranger, to my children, yes, but lacking love. Sacrificial love. Transactional "love", yes. Conditional "love", definitely. Strategic "love", yes! Protective "love", of course. Then Corinthians 13 hits me with a right and a left jab. Love is... I was familiar with it, but if ever I thought about it and how it applied to my life, it was only to measure how he loved me. And in that case, yes! You have been patient, kind, not proud, not boastful or rude, and not selfish in any way. You are not easily angered, although I have given you much to be angry about. You have been quick to forgive, but of course, I should have known my words leave wounds. You had never given up hope, and you had not quit, but your love for me ended. I go through the list, and today, I apply it to myself. First, the stab to my spirit, *you can speak different languages, you can have gifts, you can have understanding and know everything there is to know, you can even have faith enough to move mountains, you can give everything away to help others, you can even sacrifice your body, but if you don't have love, this is all worthless (1 Corinthians 13:1-3).* Ouch!

- I pray for courage to pray this prayer… "Let me, Lord see me through your eyes. Amen".
- I practice patience, no.
- I practice kindness, sometimes.
- I am not jealous. Yay! Something I'm not is jealous. Redemption!
- I am not proud. No need to waste time on this one. Proud is my first name.
- I am not rude. Pause… I Ponder. Does my quick wit count as rude?
- I am not selfish. Even now, I can't see me as the Lord sees me. Yes, okay, I am.
- I am not easily angered. If Proud is my first name, Anger has been my middle name.
- I don't keep records of wrong. What? Is an imprint on my brain a record?
- I'm happy with the truth. Always, of course, but my truth.
- I never give up on people. Of course, I do.
- I never stop trusting. I never stop trusting because I don't trust to begin with.

- I never lose hope. I never had hope to lose.
- I never quit. Does not quitting on myself count?

This Lord, is how you have loved me through my mess. This Lord is how he has loved me through my hurts and disappointments. The wounds he has not inflicted but has paid the price for. And then, the Lord, in His infinite mercy and grace and love, removed the scales from my eyes. The strength, the control, the mouth that gave voice to every egotistical thought, the pride that flared when it feared hurt or disappointment, the lack of vulnerability, and the hardened heart was to protect that little girl. The little girl I thought I had left behind. The miles I set between the place of my birth and the family I would birth were not enough distance or time to save that little girl. I had found my voice, but the words that came from my lips were not for my husband. The wounds I carried were not inflicted by his hands; he did not separate my soul from my spirit. He is not my abuser. I weep. He did not rob me of my innocence. I wail for the time wasted. I feel my anger rise within me for allowing this man to get inside my psyche and damage a man who had loved me. I was damaged, and he loved me. He has not been a perfect man, he has his own flaws and his own hurts and traumas, and through them, he has managed to love me and care for me and make me feel secure. He has placed my needs even before his own. He has paid the price for my traumas. Yes. Independence and strength were my chant, my tongue my sharpest weapon, showing no vulnerability was my survival. I was fighting my cause, defending my position, engaging in survival-like combat, but it was not him I should have been fighting. He paid the price, and when the price got to be too high, he left the fight. A fight that was never his. It was mine, and it became ours. We just didn't see it. All my life, I've been fighting not to become like my mom, that I became unlovable like my dad. Prideful, insensitive, yielding my strength. I am exhausted now. I surrender it all. I fall to my knees. I sob. I see you, little girl; set your weapons down and be healed. You survived it. It is now time for you to thrive. I question my loving God, Isn't it too late? Isn't the damage too much to overcome? The hurt is deep, Lord. Isn't it too much even for you to heal the hurts I've inflicted? I saw, once again, the shards, shreds, and mess that unhealed wounds leave in its path. I had been in a season of drought and floods because I had not seen that I was the storm. Much like you cannot see the forest through the trees, I could not see the storm that was brewing within me. Distance did not and could not heal the hurts I carried. I cried for the young lady, who was blossoming and tried to tape down her breast so that they would not show and hoped against hope that I could make them stop growing. I sob for the girl who was too young to be left behind, with no power, scared in the dark but still at peace, knowing that her dad would not be there to harm her. I sobbed because my pride had been my security, and although it brought destruction, it would be hard to give it up. I sobbed for my best friend and her painful journey. I cried finally for my brother, who died, and I never shed a tear for. That afternoon, on the floor, I cried until I had no tears left to cry, and I died to my survival self and began the fight against my ego, my pride, and the sharpest weapon in my arsenal, my tongue.

The young woman had a beautiful figure and was lovely to look at.
Esther 2:7

The Weather

A stormy season with rough seas and unexpected, and sometimes, relentless waves; that have caused my ship to feel weary, bruised, and battered.

I must weather the storm… and learn that the strength is not in the ship but in Him who built it.

In the expansive ocean, my ship appears insignificant and leads me to fear, but trust in the loving hands and the craftsmanship of the builder – provides peace.

I am grateful that I am not a boat, lost and wandering in the leisurely pleasures of what appear to be calm streams, but that the Almighty Lord built me to be a Ship that can weather the storm.

For amid the storm, my ship has been humbled, strengthened, and redeemed!

The weather forecast is unknown, but I am grateful for the storm, for, through it, I have found that this ship is but a vessel that leads me to eternity.

7

Noticing the Breeze

During the heatwave, I learned to appreciate a cool breeze. As that teenager, who knew she had had enough abuse. I knew whom to go to. I knew whom to tell, and he was a breeze in the heatwave. By the time I was a senior in high school, I had lived on my own. My mother and younger siblings had packed and moved five hours away to be with my father after his release from jail. Although I had no electricity, and little food, only the one that my grandmother would bring by every few days, even in that Texas heat, I was glad to get some peaceful and uninterrupted sleep. I had been shuffled to a couple of foster homes after my father had been released, and Social Services discovered my father had returned to our home. In that senior year, I think he was concerned I would give up before I graduated high school. He took a huge risk for himself personally, his marriage, and his livelihood. I heard his wife scream in opposition. I can't say that I blame her. They had a comfortable upper-middle-class life. Why would he risk that? But he did, and I know he was the breeze that lifted this leaf from the pile of leaves. I am forever deeply grateful to him for taking that risk and growing that confidence in me that made me believe I was worth that risk. As I made decisions in my life, it was him I did not want to disappoint. It is my graduation picture with him that I treasure most. I'm glad we kept in touch over the years. I was happy to hear the pride in his voice as I updated him in on my travels, family, and work. As his life came to an end, I was grateful for the opportunity to speak to his wife and hear her say, "He always talked about you and was so proud of you. You are one he never forgot and held close to his heart. I think it is best you don't speak to him anymore. His dementia is bad, and he won't remember you now, but I'm sure he would want you to know that." I don't know how many of his students kept in touch with him. I don't know if she would say that to other students. It didn't matter, I knew what he meant in my life, and I knew what I heard in his voice in the conversations we had had over the years. That breeze changed the trajectory of my life, and I am forever grateful to Col. EC.

Many years later. I interviewed for a position I desperately wanted and thought I would be a great fit for. I knew I had much to learn, but I was confident in my ability to contribute to it. It was with a foreign company with a different culture and long workdays. I was surprised and disappointed when I did not get it. Not because I thought I was the most knowledgeable or qualified, but because I knew that the interview went well, and I had walked out confident the position was mine. I promptly wrote a letter of thanks for their consideration and expressed my interest in any future positions with the company. Two weeks later, I received a call with a voice on the other end of the phone, "the person we hired did not work out, and we would like to make you an offer." The offer was more than I had ever earned to that point. The position was fast-paced, I learned a lot, and it was more rewarding and thrilling than I had ever anticipated. That was another breeze. It opened doors to new worlds, a new language, and a new culture, and it connected me with people around the world. A wonderful and welcomed breeze. Then came the time when my boss was offered a major promotion that would have him managing the New York City branch. He said, "I'd like to take you with me." The money was great! And NYC was the place to be. Of course, I would take it. I went home and shared the news with my husband. I said, "I was offered this position, and I am leaving. He asked, "And me and the girls? You know I can't leave. I have a contract that will keep me here." "I know I said, but I thought about it, the money is great, and it's NYC! I can't pass up on it." He continued, "one day, when I'm done with my contract, we will focus on your career; for now, you know I have to do this." Two weeks later, I turned in my resignation.

It was not required that I travel to NYC, I could have stayed at the branch I was at, but my spirit lead me in a different direction. A direction that with his travels and the demands on his time, was best suited for our family. This was a well-disguised breeze; I was serving people instead of profits.

A few years later, serving communities with limited resources, I was paid less money, but the work was more rewarding. However, some of these places and non-profits do good work, but practices are informed mostly from a place of superiority and sympathy, not empathy. Most importantly, they function with minimal or superficial accountability. The more depressed the community, the more they function like a dysfunctional family. Houses are turned into offices because of the limited availability of office buildings, which lends itself to turning offices into places where inappropriate and less-than-professional behavior occurs. Challenged and disgusted by it. I spoke to my husband, and he supported my decision to leave and stay home. Things for our young family were tight then. It was during those times that we learned that the people that grow to depend on you continue to demand of you, regardless of the changes in our circumstances. Through it, we learned to begin to say no to our families and to make sure our family was taken care of and cared for first, a needed breeze.

The next breeze came in the form of an offer to a position I knew I could do and contribute to, but it would be a learning curve to learn the medical language I would have to learn. Once hired, I worked hard to learn quickly but questioned myself. You were my loudest cheerleader, but I doubted. My supervisor at the time believed in my ability to learn. Patiently guided me and taught me what she could, and provided lots of material for me to read. Once again, the pay was better, but the job provided an opportunity to grow my confidence. This opportunity, and her mentorship, changed the trajectory of my life at a time when I needed to grow and challenge myself. I had planned to settle our family somewhere other than the state we were residing in then, but I grew to enjoy the position and the possibilities. We decided we would stay and make this home, even though you were overseas on another extended assignment, an unexpected breeze.

It was my position as a manager that I found most rewarding, the opportunity to impact policy and community. It was this position that grew my confidence and skills, the position I relied on and sought respite in when this season in my life was happening. With a new Director in place, figuring out how to put me in my place. She said, "I have written you up for…" I did not hear her words; whatever it was, I knew it was not true. She had been trying for a couple of years to trip me up, so I had been on alert. She could not question my work ethic, dedication, or the significant progress we had made under my leadership and with extensive collaboration. As she placed the paper on my side of the table, I heard her say, "Just sign there; it is not saying you agree, just that you acknowledge receiving it", I refused. A couple of months before this exchange, I had received an email from a colleague. Review the attachment. I think this is a perfect position for you. I thought, but I'm not looking for another position. I know I'm miserable now, but I love my work. I will just wait my director out. She will leave, and I will still be here. So, I quickly skimmed through the responsibilities of the position and thought, whoever gets this position will have a great opportunity to do innovative things. I will save it for a colleague I think could rise to this opportunity. Around the same time, I had submitted a leave form for one day off from all the leave I had accumulated over the years because I enjoyed my position and there was always much to be done. I had been taking a day here and there to drive my friend to her chemotherapy appointments. This particular day off would be for a surgery scheduled early on a Friday morning. I would only need to take that Friday off. The leave was approved about two weeks prior to the day. As I prepared my things to walk out of work the day before the surgery, the director quickly peaks her head in my office, "I need you here tomorrow. I've canceled your leave." I had not made her aware of my friend's condition or why I needed to take leave. I replied, "I won't be here tomorrow." She repeated, "Your leave is canceled." I repeated, "It doesn't matter to me. I am telling you that I won't be here tomorrow, and you do what you must do." I was upset when I got home that evening. Hoping I could vent to someone, but in this season, my Lavandi is ill, my confidant busy with his divorce, my job was in shambles, the pain in my back can only be managed with cortisone injections, and you and I could not be further apart. So, I pack my things in preparation for my trip, and then I get the phone call. It's Lavandi on the line, and she says, "My surgery has been canceled. They will reschedule it for another time. I will let you know when it is scheduled." What? No! I protest to myself. I say, "Well, I can come anyway and just…" She interrupts me. "No," she says. "I'm tired, and I will be sleeping most of the time. I would rather you wait to come until I need you. It will be rescheduled soon, she says, and I'll need you here then, ok?" I reluctantly agree.

My pride flares, but my Christ does too. There is an internal battle raging in me. Pride chanting a battle cry. I can't show up at that job tomorrow. I just can't! She will think I'm there because of her threat. She will think I gave in. I will not go. I will not. My spirit battling, right or righteousness, what is my choice? The next morning, I feel like I will pass out as my pride dies a slow death. I get dressed, I'm upset, and I pout and fuss the entire forty-five-minute drive to work. Sure enough, no sooner do I sit at my desk, does the director walk past my door, peeking her head in to say, "good morning," with a smirk on her face, "I see you decided to come in". My pride with that sharp tongue wants to say, "oh, it's not because of you or your demands or your threats; it is only because my friend's surgery got canceled", and instead I smile and stay silent, but the battle going on internally is raging, and I'm losing, and Christ is winning. I drink water and swallow my words and choke on my pride.

The following Wednesday, I was written up again. Once again, I know my work ethic. I know I'm not driven by emotions. I know my commitment to my work. Once again, I hear her say, "sign here". Once again, I refuse. She says, "are you sure you just don't want to go ahead and resign." The answer comes from my lips, but I don't know whom this person speaking is, "you do what you must do. I will be here until God decides, not a minute later and not a minute sooner. My future is not in your hands or mine. I am not worried," I say, with confidence and not pride, "if you are done, I will return to my desk. I have plenty of work to do". I stand and walk out, wondering who was speaking back there. That evening after work, as I drove to a mid-week service, I answer a phone call. I heard the voice say, "Dr. so and so, and Dr. so and so, and I were so eager to offer you the position as soon as you walked out of the interview, but we had to deliberate. As you know, the position requires a PHD, but we are confident that you have what it takes, and we want you to join us. I sent you an offer letter; please review it closely. If you object to anything, please let us know. We really want to have you leading this project. Do you think you can get back to me this evening?" I pull off the highway, and find a parking lot. Open my email and read the offer letter multiple times. It was almost twice as much as I was currently earning, and the benefits exceeded my current ones. After making sure my eyes don't deceive me. I call her back. "I accept," I say. She said, "Great! When can you start?" I explained that I really was not looking for another job or looking to leave my current position, so I had much to do to prepare and asked if I could have about six weeks. She agreed and then said, "You have a budget to hire your own team. You can also decide if you want to come into the office, find an office closer to home, or work from home. I know one of the things you said you did not like about your current position was the drive downtown because of the traffic and not really being able to predict when you would make it in. So, it is not necessary for you to come in. Just let us know where you want to work from." This cannot be happening. Is this true? Am I dreaming? A breeze I needed and would come to value in my life more than anyone could have imagined. The next day, I walked in and turned in my resignation to the HR department. This was an effort to keep my pride in check so as to not gloat to the director. She soon stops by my office. "I saw your resignation letter." A smirk on her face. “I see you’ve decided to leave.” A grin. “I’m sure eventually you will find another position better suited for you.” I smile, bringing death to my pride, and with joy in my heart, I respond, “I’m sure I will.” She immediately raised the stakes, put pressure for me to leave earlier, especially after she denied my leave for my friend’s rescheduled surgery. I had no choice but to change my resignation date from six weeks to four. I rushed to create a book with instructions for the next person and rushed to clean out my office. Even four weeks was too long for her incessant tactics. I no longer had the energy or interest to engage her in her misery; my priority was my Lavandi. Since she had denied my leave, I had to use my sick time to drive Lavandi to her chemotherapy treatments. Even my exit was made difficult, challenging my remaining leave days, the payout, challenging the use of my sick days. She brought in a calendar of days she claimed I did not turn in leave slips and days I was off that I did not call. My payout for all these days accumulated would be significantly less than I anticipated. I had no energy left to give over to her and these games. I called my new boss and let her know that I would be available to start earlier than I thought. I was prepared to be in the office for orientation for the first weeks or months, and I was concerned and nervous that Lavandi’s surgery would be scheduled during my orientation time. I was then informed that it was up to me to schedule my orientation for one day a week in the office as best it worked for my schedule and hers. Wow! She was serious that it was what worked best for me. I had given her an answer. I would work from home. Less than two months later, my friend had her surgery. Since I worked from "home," I was able to work from Lavandi's hospital room every day. There was much to read and many protocols and procedures to develop. I would get those done while she slept. In between times, in the brief times when she was awake and not in pain, Lavandi and I would talk. I was there when she finally was strong enough to get out of bed and have her first real shower. I was there the first time she saw herself in the mirror and burst into tears, to see her body and recognize the part of her body that was no longer there. Once discharged, I was in her home, where her husband had turned her living room into her makeshift hospital room and where I could sleep in a cot next to her. I could be with her at night as she screamed in agony. The sign was that it was time for her next medication. A painful breeze, yes, it was a breeze because the Lord opened the door to what I needed at the time and what I would treasure for a lifetime. A new and exciting position that combined community with policy and policy with collaboration and collaboration with practice. A position that provided the space, time, and freedom to be present with her. I could not relieve her pain, but I could be part of her journey. I could try to make her comfortable. I could clean her up and let her keep her dignity. All these are a welcomed breeze prompted by an unexpected storm.

Yes, it was a season. A season of drought and floods but a season that brought some relief. Yes, I left that job, but it was like neither of us imagined at the time; it was better than I could have imagined or prayed for or could have made happen in my own strength or will—the timing, perfect.

In this new position, I found a refreshing breeze; humanity, compassion, and a group of purpose-driven women, committed to their area of expertise and always working to fit perfectly into the larger puzzle. This is where egos came to die so that humanity could thrive, where failure was seen as an opportunity for innovation, and the lessons learned informed the next plan. The foundation was integrity and respect. I typically worked fourteen-to-sixteen-hour days and traveled extensively, but no matter how long or how hard I worked, I knew my boss worked longer and harder. She was mission-driven but encouraged a work-life balance. I remember when I accepted the position, I talked it over with my husband, and we agreed I would stay in this position for five years. I would then take a leap of faith and step out on my own. *"I will lay a table before your enemies," (Psalm 2:5)* that is what scripture says. I remember the day my new boss called and said your old boss called and has received some funding that requires that she works with us on a project, and I'd like you to meet with her and get information on what she needs and let me know if you think we should work with them and how. I smiled, a breeze. Sitting across from her, I chose grace. I practiced grace. I would not shame my God. I remained professional, and most importantly, righteousness won out as more of my pride died.

Five years later, it was time for me to move on. Through tears, both my boss and I knew it was time. "You have outgrown us. You are meant for a bigger stage. I wonder whether you feel that. Do you know that? I feel like we are holding you back. Please let me know if and how I can best help you with that. I can make phone calls. I think you would be great at this position and can best influence policy at the state level. Let me know if you are interested, and I will place a phone call." How did she know it was my five-year mark? How did she know I had been feeling her exact words? I thought about what she said, and it was an interesting but safe offer. It would not be stepping out on faith. A few weeks later, I returned to her and said, "thank you, but no thank you." I had nothing secure; I had no other position or income. It would just be faith, but I had learned in this five-year season that faith, properly placed, not in me or my abilities or what I see or anticipate, is all I needed when I placed it in God. She said, "I don't want to lose you, but I know holding you back is not the right thing to do." I knew it but leaving an awesome team of driven women was the hardest thing I've ever done in my professional career. I said to her, "I will close out the year here." New year, new beginnings.

As I prepared to launch my own business, the exact date all things were set to go, the announcement from the Government came—quarantine. No meeting in enclosed spaces, no more than 10 people, preferably five. The next two years, so much unknown, so much unrest, so many people dying, and so many protesting. All I had to survive on was faith. In this season I receive an unexpected check. An audit was conducted, and I was owed backpay for my leave days from all those years ago. Wow!

The Col., K-San, PTD, SM (the stranger), and KG, the breezes in my life; with each breeze, I found reprieve and found myself lifted and carried in a different direction and each time landing in more fertile land. But to be lifted, I recognize I first had to surrender. Surrender my plans, my ideas, my wit, my pride, and silence my tongue, so that His breeze could carry me.

Then Jesus said to his disciples, "Whoever wants to be my disciple must deny themselves and take up their cross and follow me."
Matthew 16:24

8

Mother Nature

My hopes and dreams were to one day be a mother. A mother to a daughter or preferably daughters. I did not pray for riches, wealth, big homes, or fancy cars. I did not pray for daughters because I needed love. I did not pray for a traditional family. I did not want to right any wrongs, I would not put that load on my daughters. Neither had I fantasized about making my daughters my friends. I wanted daughters I would love unconditionally—daughters that would feel safe and secure. I wanted to mold girls into women that were empowered. Women that could walk confidently into this world created for men—women who are free to make their own choices. I wanted to raise little girls that would know no hunger, no need, no lack, not of things, but of self. Women who did not find a need for validation from men or anyone. Women that understood their self-worth. Women, I would like as friends, bosses, and compassionate servants. I wanted to mold girls that I could see myself admiring as women. The Lord answered my prayers this time and exceeded my dreams.

The privilege of my life has been to be part of our three daughters' lives and to have each of them mold me into the mother they need. I am far from the mother I imagined in my fantasy world that I would be, but I became a constant student. One day they might discuss their experiences as my daughters, and one thing I know for sure they will say, because they say it now, to me. After all the apple does not fall far from the tree. They say they wish they had seen me cry. Not because they wished for me any pain or suffering but because they sometimes experienced pain, suffering, loss, and hurt from breakups and life in general. Since they had never seen me cry, they felt that they could not. My failure to be vulnerable had not only impacted my relationship with my husband, but it had prevented our daughters from sharing their pain and vulnerabilities. They are grateful, however, and express, "You raised us to be good men, not emotional, more emotional than you, but still not showing much emotion." They are also not physically demonstrative of emotion, so say their partners, and each, of course, lay that directly on my doorstep. I know they are right, but at the doorstep, it stays. I do not internalize that. From my perspective, they can choose differently, so although I have been an influence, as adults, they can make different choices. For today I take joy in watching them be adult women that I like. Women that are secure enough in our love for them that they can share what they want about themselves with us, the good, the bad, and the ugly. I take great pleasure and comfort in watching them grow, each of them so different from the other, with their unique strengths and weaknesses, complex but confident in their complexity and striving. Always searching to be a better version of themselves. They are women who seek our advice and respect our experiences but do not need our approval. They are considerate of us as their parents and respect us as people. Each of them, more emotional than I understand sometimes, but I secretly admire that about them. It informs their kindness and the caring women they are in what sometimes can be a cold world. My proudest moments are when they are quick-witted with me. I just never imagined anyone would be quicker than I with wit, and when they get one in, I puff up with pride. They are by no means perfect, but they are students and women I would not mind being friends with. I take pleasure and pride in knowing that they are each on their own journey, forming their own path, and I celebrate that as they seek, they are seeking better versions of themselves, not better versions of me.

God's gift to me was molding me into the joys of motherhood that come with having a partner in life. I did not do it my way, and I did not do it alone like I had imagined it. I remember the first time we were pregnant. Once again, my pride was at the ready even in this moment of joy, especially once I learned we were having a daughter. I told you that you were free to leave, and your purpose had been fulfilled. Once again, your love for me and our family was steadfast. You stayed. Your presence, your involvement, your provision, and your expressions of love, after our first, second, and third daughters provided stability and the support I needed to grow in confidence as a mother and my ability to enjoy every phase and stage of motherhood. It was divine intervention that brought you to me, and it was grace that kept you with our family.

In my adult years, I've come to the realization that my hope for daughters was to right the wrongs of man but also to love from power and not from resilience, like my mother. I wanted to share the love that my mother poured on me, as best as a teenage mother with limited options and even fewer resources could, giving birth to me at just eighteen years old. By the time my own mother was twenty years old, she was a mother to seven children. Her oldest child being only eight years her junior, and only one year in between her six older children. As a child, I did not pay attention to the close interval between my mother's age and my oldest sibling's. I never questioned it. It is because in all areas, my mother acted as their parent, and in every aspect, my brothers acted as her biological children. She washed, cleaned, cared for them, and walked them to school, just as she did for me. I did not notice any difference in her love for them or notice a difference in their love of her. My six older brothers and, later, my older sister had been brought to live with us a few years after my father's divorce from his first wife and a year into my parent's marriage. Their mother had pulled up, parked on the road in front of the house my parents shared, opened the door, pointed them towards the house, and rode off. The next time anyone would lay eyes on her would be fifteen years later at my oldest brother's funeral. He longed to see her face in life. He would say, if only to know what she looks like. That was not to be, but in his death, after much encouragement, she showed up for fifteen minutes. Mothers, their absence is sometimes as powerful as their presence.

I knew my mother loved me, and I also knew I did not want to grow up to be like her. I am grateful to her for fighting the good fight for my sister and I to be able to go to school like my brothers did. I saw my father's blows and heard her screams. I learned to recognize her different cries; some were from physical pain, and others from suffering and disappointment. Her voice was never silent when she disagreed with my father, who would loudly and strongly voice his opinion about us not needing an education to go have babies and be wives. She would voice her opinion and immediately hurry us off to school. I did not have to imagine the punishment she suffered for back talking my father because I would see the bruises.

As my older brothers became teenagers, they started to speak up for our mother. The response from our father was violent, particularly when my father was choking my mother, and my brothers broke down the bedroom door to save her. I remember we managed to find safety in an orange orchard in a van that served as accommodations for eight of us.

My mother raised ten children, seven of whom she did not give birth to but loved all the same. These memories of a teenage mother, resilient, sometimes even defiant, to her fourteen years older husband's anger cultivated the gratitude and admiration that allowed me to forgive her shortcomings.

I believe my mother did not know what my father did to me as a child. What I do know is that when I was fifteen years old, my mother knew. She knew when they arrested, convicted, and took him to jail. She knew it when she allowed him to come back home to live with us after his release, and I was taken to live in a foster home. She knew it when they moved five hours away, leaving me behind to live on my own. My grandmother lived a few blocks away, and she would check on me and make sure I had food to eat. I supposed my mother and grandmother agreed to this arrangement.

I also understood that my mother was a housewife and did not get paid for her work and still had my two younger siblings to care for. She left, not because she chose him over me, is what I've told myself, but because this was the only way to provide for my two youngest brothers. I imagine I would choose differently. The truth is that I was a witness to her life but did not and have not lived her life. The truth is that I have never walked in her shoes. The truth is that I believe she did the best she could in her circumstances. I know that she loved me then, and she loves me now. I am the mother I am today in honor of the mothers of the past. Those who did not have choices, voices, or value, in a world created for men.

Mothers are an influential and formidable force. My husband's mother is no different—a woman who had to make tough choices in tough circumstances. She had dreams as a young woman, I am sure, dreams that would not become a reality. She had to provide for her children's physical needs or care for her children's emotional needs, both were not an option, and that leaves scars on a mother's heart. As a teenage mother herself at fourteen years old, her skills and education limited. However, her ability and determination, admirable. She made a life for a family of seven and even managed to purchase a home. Home-ownership is the American dream that is denied to many with limited education, and she made it happen. Our customs and values are different, but I understand how her life and experiences inform them, and that understanding informs why when she comes into my home, it is hers to do as she wishes.

It informs why when my husband gets a raise, I suggest to my husband that we raise what we financially provide for her. Sending my husband to her on Mother's Day, without me joining him, is how I acknowledge and honor her story. I don't want to be a distraction or compete for his time. I want her to feel special, and I want his attention and focus on her.

The first time I heard her voice was on the phone, my husband and I were newlyweds. She called to advise me that just because her son was married to me did not mean he could not keep in touch with his female friends back home. She rattled off the names of women that she thought he would want to keep in touch with. It took me a minute as I tried to recall where I had heard those names before. Ah, yes! The love drawer—the letters, photos, gifts, and notes had these names on them. My response was as cold as her advice, and I let her know that neither her nor I would be making that decision. The lines were drawn; we ended up on opposite sides.

The next time we exchanged words was when we met in person, in her home, clearly on her turf and on her terms. The 11 ½ x 8" framed picture, the same picture I had seen years earlier in my husband's love drawer, sat on top of her television in the living room. No less beautiful than what I remembered. In her voice, a warning, "That is Cindy, she is the one he lived with before he left. She is a close friend of our family, and she is always welcomed here. I'm letting you know in case she comes over for a visit". It was obvious she was disappointed that her son did not marry her. At that moment, I wanted to tell her that we were on the same side; I too, was disappointed that he did not marry her. I wanted to tell her that I tried to encourage reconciliation. I really did; it just didn't work. But I was not sure if that would bring us together or tear us further apart, so I kept silent. This once again solidified that we were not on the same side and would remain on opposing sides for years to come. Only twenty years later would I learn her perspective on the story. As she shared, "the first time you came to my house, you called your mom on the phone and explained that you felt like a stranger in my house or town. You remember that?" I didn't, but I believe her. I was in a new city, in a home-alone all day, as my husband went missing without a phone call and she went to work. I can see that phone call happening exactly as she described it. She goes on, "I didn't appreciate that." I respond, "Wow! You've held on to that this long. That is where our problems stem from? You should've mentioned it before. I believe what you described is totally possible, and I'm sorry." Then a litany of reasons of what was wrong about me; my parenting, my beliefs that I'm better, if I visit them with my husband if I don't go visit, keeping our daughters from forming a relationship with them, etc. "We love your family, your brothers, your mother… They are all so nice." After a few minutes, I would stop listening. I understood. I had heard it before. In our brief exchanges, it was always the same. I empathized, but I neither agreed nor disagreed, and that is the problem. I place no value in their opinions or thoughts of me. Collectively, as a family, and individually, their thoughts and opinions did not influence who or how I was. I wish I could have cared enough or had built a bond so that I could take the time to explain that it was not them I did not value, it was their opinion, but it was only because that is not how I live my life. I care about feedback about my work as a strategy for improvement, but for me to consider an observation of me, not an emotional and biased opinion, I must have a relationship. It's not you; it's me, is what I wanted to say, but not as an apology, because not internalizing people's opinions of me had been my safety net. I wanted for them peace and understanding. I didn't think she, or the family, would understand and once again kept silent, and we would remain on opposing sides.

It did not help our relationship to have a husband that placed his mother on a pedestal, like many sons do, right up there with Mary, the mother of Christ. This position yields a type of unquestionable power and influence. I understand the influence and even the power of a parent, the part that I was incapable of understanding was the "unquestionable" because, as a curious person, question is part of my practice that informs my lived experience. He worshipped her like a Mona Lisa, and this ensured that I would always be the disobedient subject for my failure to show the same unquestionable reverence.

I was not capable of not questioning. It was a survival skill I had learned at a young age. I was certainly defiant, but the value or lack of value placed on me by my father because I was a girl taught me not to place value on my gender. I joined the drill team, R.O.T.C., and other clubs. I traveled with teams, and I gave my phone number to boys. I would hear the rumors from my maternal grandmother; oh, she is jumping around so much her hymen is going to break, and she will no longer be considered a virgin. I dispelled those rumors. Too much value was placed on my virginity. I hated it. Maybe because that ship had sailed, and not in the way I would have chosen. It all seemed hypocritical, and so I placed no value in the rumors. A few summers, we had the opportunity to visit with my paternal grandmother, about five hours away from where we lived. My paternal aunts lived in the area. I remember as my sister was pampered and showered on with praise and outings, I was relegated to dishes and making certain I felt their rejection. To be fair, I don't think they disliked me, they disliked my mom, and as a result, it was taken out on me. I didn't get hit; I was rejected intentionally. These little biddies did not know that I understood what they thought. I must be treated favorably by my mom because she birthed me and not my sister and they, in their eyes, were setting things right. Since I found a way to justify their behavior, I did not internalize their treatment. It was not me; it was them. The more incidents like this I experienced, the more I could justify them and the less harm they caused. I don't really think they meant any real harm, and today, I am grateful for it. I internalize nothing and only consider criticism as an opportunity to reflect, find the strategy, and improve, if, and this is a big if, only if you have earned my respect. That is difficult to do. I'm not easily impressed, not with degrees, fame, status, position, title, beauty, or any superficial things like that. I am impressed by integrity, character, authenticity, empathy; a life lived in grace. I am not only impressed but I am also intrigued by people with those characteristics. I am curious and eager to learn from people with character, people who seek purpose and not position, influence and not necessarily leadership, and humanity over ego.

Much of what I see in us is informed by our childhood experiences. The experiences he lacked with his own parents make him a present, engaged and loving father. His need to be seen was informed by the little boy who needed to be emotionally cared for and valued. To this day, he is a dedicated and doting son, providing for his mother's emotional, financial, and physical needs. Always thoughtful and careful to affirm her position. While she, on the other hand, claimed not to know him.

I know this is disappointing and painful for him, but he keeps it silent and even attempts to justify it because of the content of his character.

My mother, his mother, our mothers, carried loads we couldn't imagine carrying. I admire their ability to carry these heavy loads, understanding that I have not walked their journey. It is these loads that burdened our childhoods and that now influence our adult lives; you needing to be seen and valued, and me needing to be heard, and both of us surviving by ignoring the needs of our childhood.

A father to the fatherless. God sets the lonely in families.
Psalms 68:5-6

9

Cold

I know when it is time. Excitement in the air around you. You are always eager to leave. Your trips meticulously planned. Your clothes and shoes carefully selected. Like a teenager preparing for prom. Your alternate phone discreetly packed. Like a kid in a candy store, giddy. You would not be denied, the sweetness of the taste and smell of new and secret encounters. The pep in your step could not be denied. You would not deny yourself these stolen moments. Eager like I had not seen in years. I remember when the newness was us and when that thirst was only for me. But I am not part of this equation, and that thirst will not be quenched by me. In its place is anger. These days, you move about and around me as if my existence suffocates you. As if I rob the very oxygen from your lungs. As the scheduled call comes at the expected time. I imagine your last call happened directly before you walked in the house. That was when you confirmed the time, but my usual weekly evening appointment is canceled. Your words seek to explain what your face has already told me. You say it's a friend. A friend you will call back later. Your friend is insistent and the phone rings again. She has clearly not been made aware of the change in my schedule. How could you, this just happened an hour before on this Wednesday night and here I am, an intruder in our home. I say, "answer the call your friend clearly has an urgent matter" and walk away giving you the time, space, and privacy that is customary of a setting for an intimate conversation. I know these calls. The calls of anticipation. The calls to make plans for when we will meet again. The calls that bring comfort to a relationship built on sand, a relationship clinging on to hope.

Predictable. You leave and my calls begin. They come early in the morning and right before my bedtime. Calculating, they've become, your departure and my 7:00 a.m. calls. When you are in town, this is our time. The time that you and I usually go for our weekend drives. Now it's time you leave her side and excuse yourself to get coffee or breakfast, or maybe you tell her you're headed for a quick jog. Although she knows it's an excuse, she lets you go. After all, this is the price for this secret exchange.

Your calls, a temperature check. An inquisition to gauge how dead or how alive we are. Good morning, babe. Where are you? "Home," I say, calming your fears that you might be found out. How are the children? "Well," I say, soothing your guilt. Then the excuses. I'm sorry I missed your call last night. I had my phone on vibrate, or the sound was turned down, or I forgot my phone in the car. Predictable, my husband, so predictable. Then you rattle off the list of things that you will be engaged in that will make you unavailable. Sometimes, my heart wishes you were less predictable and more creative. Maybe you no longer care to be thoughtful, or maybe I never expected more. Once again, releasing you from your guilt, I say, "I won't call you that way; I won't interrupt your day or your plans. You call me when you have time." The calls always came, every morning right after your escape and every evening right before you flew onto the web for the night.

As time goes on, the calls that should bring you joy bring you stress. Where does that confidence go when you feel the need to hide? Where is your courage to defend that which you believe to be real, true, and only for you?

I wonder, where is my anger? Where is my fury? Where is my heart to care for what I witness? Why can I see you drive away from home, your home, our home, our family, and be pleased to see you giddy? Is it love, or is it surrender? Maybe it is the remorse of knowing that it is not her that takes you from me, but it is I who surrenders you to her. It is you that drives away, but it is I that created the distance. The miles between you and I, I painstakingly laid brick by heavy brick. I wonder, will this be the end of the journey for us, or do I have the strength to build a U-turn on this fast-moving one-direction highway?

I check the fireplace in our house. I check it often. It seems to function properly, but it does not raise the temperature in our home and does nothing for the temperature in our hearts. I am reminded of an old saying, where there was once fire, a spark remains. I pray it is true. Although sometimes I see a glimmer of a spark, the darkness is also very real and intense.

I cook your dinner and serve your plate. Cold, your response. Occasionally our fingers touch, and my hands are eager for the warmth of your touch. Your reflexes were quick, but the pain lingers, nonetheless. I grit and grin as we graze past each other. As you come and go, I stay occupied with the business of the house, the kids, the bills, and the job. These days, I am grateful for the moments of escape. Maybe I should not be, maybe I am a cold woman for using these moments that I care for my friend as my moments to gather strength.

Do you not see, or do you not care about the weariness in my spirit? The weight of it all. I might lose you and her forever—the friend of my youth, my loyal confidant. Closer she is to me than my own blood. She knows the worst of me and finds the best in me. Not once in twenty-six years has she leveraged my weaknesses. We've disagreed on much, even our marriages, children, and faith. We have different interests in life. How can two women, born on the same day and year, with four hours difference between us, me being the oldest as she laughingly liked to remind me, be so different and love each other so deeply.

She, like you, an example of love, sincere friendship, and deep intimacy. She was my soul sister until her last breath. I had prepared myself that morning to meet her request, a hospital happy hour. She could not leave the hospital, and she said, "Bring happy hour to me." Just like we used to do it, she had instructed me. Happy Hour, yes, that was always us, grazers. We would usually meet ½ way from where we live, but sometimes I would visit her in her city, or she'd visit me in my town, but always grazing. We never ordered individual meals. We ordered a variety of appetizers so that we could sit, relax, enjoy a drink or two and try every appetizer that covered our table. On her visits to my town, she would always have the trunk of her SUV packed with all types of goodies, baked goods, cheese dips, and every type of snack the kids were sure to love, and every type of finger food we would partake of that evening. She brought the homemade goodies, and I brought the drinks. Back when we were newlyweds and young mothers, we started feeling giddy and accomplished when we went from sharing a wine cooler to sharing a four-pack of Bartles & Jayme's wine coolers. We really thought we were doing something then. As we matured, so did our choice of drinks. A berry sangria was our drink of choice now. Any cocktail semi-sweet and fruity was just right for us. Sometimes I would be able to talk her into having a shot of tequila or two.

The night before our happy hour in the hospital, I cooked her favorite cheese dip from her recipe. I was happy to do it. Happy to get back to one of our favorite routines together, grazing, sipping, and chatting. We would chat for hours, and laugh mostly at ourselves as wives, as parents, the younger us when we thought we knew everything and realized now we knew nothing. I was giddy because her request for a happy hour must be a good sign, right? I was pleased with how her recipe turned out. Maybe one day, I would be able to make the most unquestionably delicious, popular, and in constant-demand finger-licking and succulent cinnamon rolls from her recipe. She would share that recipe with nobody except her daughter and one of my daughters. I pack the wine that has been chilling overnight, the appetizers packed in containers that we would heat in the microwave on our arrival, the napkins, the small plates, the tiny forks just like she liked, always meticulous, always thoughtful, that was her way. I even bought a sign, a small chalkboard in a frame that I wrote "Happy Hour" on. The four of five, I count as my daughters and my reliable squad, (3 daughters I birthed and one of the two, I chose), had wanted to go for a visit for a while, and we all agreed this was a perfect time. We, together, would set the vibe for a perfect happy hour, dawn our hospital gowns, unpack the wine glasses, uncork the wine, and set out the appetizers. We got on the road early that morning, aiming to beat the D.C. traffic and arrive at about 7 or 7:30 that morning.

I learned of the mercy of God that morning during our "happy" hour. As I walked into her room with my bags, announcing my visit and preparing to make memories that would hopefully make her forget about the pain for one hour, I walked into an unexpected scene. A medical team was working hard to revive her. A doctor with hands on her chest turns to me and screams, "are you her next of kin?" I am cold; I am frozen still. The shouts come again, "are you her next of kin?" My head races to find an answer; yes, yes, I am her closest next of kin, the one who loves her more than a sister can. I am the one who has driven her to her appointments, the one who has sat next to her while the chemo is pumped in her veins, the one who has bathed her and dressed her. Yes, I am the one that slept in her makeshift bedroom that was once the living room where we enjoyed movies, grazed over appetizers, and where we created moments that I now desperately pray for. I am the one who gave her the medicines that in the end, would not subside her pain or soothe her agonizing screams. Yes, by that measure, I am her closest next of kin. I am the one who knows her deepest secrets and her biggest fears. I am the one who knows her pains and joys of motherhood. I know her deepest losses. I remember her pain at the rapid loss of her mother to breast cancer. I remember her sacrifice when she interrupted her own chemotherapy treatment to rush to her father's side at his lung cancer diagnosis. Yes, I remember her struggles to conceive the second time around. I know about the time we were stuck in a snowstorm together with our infant daughters, born two weeks apart. I remember the boredom that took us to the snow-covered streets. The two of us, unable to drive a stick shift car, found ourselves sliding down a mountain that had taken us more than an hour to drive up. We had matching outfits, for God's sake! The madness and rush of the nurses bring me back to the present. "Where is her next of kin?" they ask. "I don't know," I answered. As I turn to look for him, he appears. "Enough," he said, "enough!" The main doctor reminds him, "If we stop now, she will die. Do you understand that?" His answer is, "Yes, but it's enough. Let her rest." My ears cannot believe what I just heard. My head spins as I see the medical team stop their exhaustive efforts. I wanted to interrupt; I wanted to say no. She said not to give up! "Don't give up on me. Don't look at me as if I'm dying. Don't stop giving me updates on life as if you are waiting for me to die. Don't let the team give up", she'd say. I replied, "I won't". She was a fighter, and we needed to stay in the fight with her, but instead, I heard, "call the time." They look at the clock on the wall. They call the time, 8:10 a.m. I am cold, frozen. On the inside, I scream,

I say, no, no, he is not her next of kin – I am – and I need you to climb back up there and bring her back. The nurses, medical team, and the betrayer walk out. I am left alone in the room, and I watch her spirit, her soul, and her breath leave her body. I run my hands through her hair; I kiss her forehead. Once again, I pray, Lord, this was not the agreement. This was not the ending we had prepared ourselves for. Sure, we prepared for a long fight, but that fight was supposed to end in victory. She was going to defeat the different types of cancers in her body. That was the agreement. I come back to the room with no choice but to accept this new reality. I remember her children. Their father was to call and summon them to the hospital. I prepare myself to be their support and strength. I walk slowly toward the waiting room. I had forgotten my squad was there, waiting on happy hour, a happy hour that would not come. They asked, and the words could not come out of my mouth, but I collapsed into their arms. A pain, a loss that cannot be explained in words. The Lord, in his mercy, gave me time to grieve, gave me time to say goodbye, and gave me the privilege to be present for her last breath. In his mercy, I was there to watch her soul and spirit separate from her body. In his mercy, he gave me the time to cry before I broke the news to her only daughter, as the father broke the news to her only son. Those days are the most painful in my life. The loss is too great to recover from in this lifetime.

The friendship is too deep to replace, and yet the very reason it is so treasured.

The coldest days of my life happened that summer.

I am hard pressed on every side, but not crushed; perplexed, but not in despair; persecuted, but not abandoned; struck down, but not destroyed.
2 Corinthians 4:8-9

10

Hot

I was secure in the way you loved me, and for over twenty years, I let myself be loved. I basked in the joy and heat of that love without ever considering if I should try to maintain it. All living things require maintenance, a little heat, and a little care. All living things require protection. Why not you? Why not us?

Some living things require time, attention, and love. And when they are as tall and handsome as you, they want and need to be noticed. I so loved the way you loved me that I forgot to ask if I loved you. Now that I see you. You are smart, courteous, thoughtful, and kind. You have provided for me a platform from which to soar. Your capacity to see me and anticipate what I needed and wanted. Your patience as you taught me about life, to show me the world through your eyes and experience. Your ability to brighten my darkest moments. Your cared to bring me back to us when I was tempted to lose myself.

Now, here I am, finding it damn near impossible to serve you a cup of coffee. Why, Lord, I asked and pleaded, pass this cup from me. I do not want to be humiliated in serving, and I do not want to be reduced to this. My hands shake, my forehead has spots of sweat, my hands are clammy, and I feel faint. I feel I will pass out. Will I be the first woman to pass out from serving her husband a cup of coffee? No, I cannot be the first woman feeling oppressed by service. I push through and add the sugar and protest. I then add the cream, and I grumble.

Why do I have to serve him coffee? He should be serving me coffee! Never mind that I don't' drink coffee. And I think of Esther and hear it in my spirit; you do it out of reverence for Christ. How is serving a cup of coffee out of reverence for Christ? I don't understand, Lord. Is he worthy? Conviction comes; what can a man do to not be worthy of one cup of coffee? A stranger is worth a cup of coffee. I climb the stairs leading to our bedroom. Step by painstaking step. A journey of a thousand steps, it seemed like to me. It is more like sixteen. Each step was painful to my soul, and my pride cried in agony; if you do this, you can never go back. No cortisone injection would cure this agony. Back to the person you know yourself to be, strong, independent, aloof, here to be served and not to serve. Why would I want to kill that person? The word says to die to self, but what if I like self? Does that apply to me too? What if I am great as I am? I am good, I am kind, and the world is lucky to have me. I am knowledgeable, wise, and. Well, before I know it, I arrived with the coffee in hand. He is clearly surprised, startled almost, by my gesture. He asks, what is this? I roll my eyes, "coffee," I respond. "Here, it's for you". He looks inside the cup and asks, "What is in it"? I respond, clearly perturbed by his cautious curiosity. He questions if it's for him. I respond, "yes", and he asks, "why"? My answer comes as cold as the coffee is by now, "I'm not doing it for you; I'm doing it out of reverence for Christ," and I turn around and briskly walk out of the room. I hear his response, "well, if it is for Christ, give it to him." My pride puffs up, oh, he clearly is not worthy of a cup of coffee, I think – this time to myself – as I storm out of the room.

As I felt like I was dying slow deaths every day at home, I would pray, "Lord, change him. Change his heart towards me". I would continue to serve him coffee. I would kick rocks rather than serve him a cold beer after work, but I would remind myself I do it in obedience to Christ. I would pray, "Lord, forgive him for denying me care or love, as you command a husband to do." I would attempt playful touches and tender kisses and would find only his cold response, even if not an outright rejection. I would continue my daily all-day prayers, "Strengthen me, Lord, for he is clearly not worthy of my service. I do it in reverence to you". As days turn into weeks, and weeks into months, "Lord, let him move out then, bring my suffering to an end". And as months turned into a year, I searched for solace in someone who once cared for me deeply. I thought I'd call him and test the waters. I needed a confidence booster. He answered, surprised at first to hear from me. I listened intently for the inflections in his voice to try and asses if he was happy to hear from me or if I was interrupting his mind, his day, or his thoughts. The first call was quick, too quick to know if there was excitement in his voice, surprise, or dread. I called the next day again. I promised myself it would be quick before I got myself in trouble. The type of trouble that would bring certain death to my marriage. Once again, I played with temptation and surrendered to the playfulness of the calls. The more I called, the more we flirted with each other the more receptive he sounded. At one point, I think he even looked forward to them. He didn't say it, but I could tell. He even asked me to call him again tomorrow. I promised I would but let him know it would have to be brief, just like all the other calls. We agreed and said our goodbyes.

At home, I continued to serve coffee. As time passed, I grumbled less and no longer felt that I would pass out. You too, did not feel the need to check your coffee before you enjoyed it, and you seemed to be enjoying it more and more each day. Maybe I was learning how to make better coffee, or maybe you were just less worried about me trying to poison you. I suppose I will never know, and that is fine by me. Days went by, and I served you a cup in bed every day, and each day the cup was warmer in temperature. So was my heart; it started to feel a flutter. I'd always cooked for you but never had I taken you a beer after work. The more I did, the more I noticed a change happening. This was not the answer to the prayers I had prayed for days, weeks, months, and years. All I had prayed for, a change of heart, less anger, a softening of the heart, a healing of hurts, had slowly happened but to me. Unbeknown to me, it was also happening for me. Is this joy I feel to see you come in from work with expectation? Is this ease, relaxation, maybe even joy I detect in that smile?

Our lives still appeared to go in separate directions. I was committed to building new friendships and relationships with my new church family. You were defiantly staying home and expressing that you would never go to this church with me. I heard your protest and continued building relationships with women who never told me what my itching ears wanted to hear. One woman in particular, the stranger I had met over coffee. She would say to me, it does not matter what I say; it only matters what Christ says.

As I sought a new life, my phone calls with this man continued. I enjoyed them more and more each day, but only Monday through Friday while he was at work. The calls started to sound and feel like the affair you were having—my own confidence growing with each phone call. Words are powerful and can transport you to beautiful spaces in your heart and mind. They can also be painful. I imagined you saying the same or similar words of affection to your spider. Here I am, also getting caught in a web or maybe laying out a web. Is this the same or different? Is mine a web of lies and deceit, or is this refreshing newness real? Why would mine be real, asks my mind to my heart; why would it be? I put common sense aside and continue down this path. As the calls become more regular and intimate, things at home begin to take a turn.

You are beginning to show some signs of a softening heart, some care, gentler now. Your trips occurring less often, and even when you take them, I am invited to join you—pride rearing its ugly head in my head. Saying no, why would I want to go now and cause myself discomfort or stress? Trips to your home had always been awkward. I had never felt welcomed. These were not trips that I enjoyed, nor did I want to put myself through. How can I save my marriage when I won't take myself to the center of the battle? Am I a coward, or am I selfish? I don't know, and I don't spend much time pondering the questions I can't answer.

Now the phone calls have progressed into requests for time together. I would ask, "Like a date? Do you want to take me on a date? "Yes." His voice was secure. "On this day and at this time." I don't think I was ready for this. I was caught off guard, but my heart skipped a beat, and now it was me who was giddy. Giddy with anticipation. Imagining myself on a date. A real date. When was the last time my husband had invited me or taken me on a date, I wondered? Back to the phone call, "Are you sure?" I ask. "Yes", came the response. I noticed the confidence in his voice, and I liked it. "I'll get the tickets," he says. "I'll make the reservations." Wow! I am surprised by his forwardness. He continues, "It is the Maxwell concert on Valentine's Day." I had to ask, "Are you sure we want to do this?" Again confident, but more eager this time. I could almost detect excitement. "I know I do. Only you know if you do." "I do" I say, surprised by my own eagerness.

At home, I had grown used to making plans alone. I would go to jazz concerts whenever I could while the girls had plans and you were away. If I knew I would be partaking in wine, I would reserve a room. The girls are now older, and you are away, I would pamper myself and take trips to the beach with two of three of my favorite items; a book, always a book, and either my favorite tea or favorite wine, depending on the time of day, sunrise or sunset. I started getting excited at the possibility of having company on these escapes. I had always enjoyed time alone, and the freedom of not being responsible for someone else, but I started to let myself dream. And I dreamt of him, his company. What could possibly go wrong?

One day as I was leaving for a concert, wearing my red shorts, white linen top, tall heels, shades, and a red sunhat, to meet some friends. You unexpectedly arrived, returning early from your trip. You asked where I was headed—a surprise in your eyes. Maybe you imagined that while you were gone on your weekend trips, I would be home curled up or with my focus on my world falling apart. I don't know. I never said, and you never asked. I suppose you did not care. Then you ask, "Can I join you?" "I'm meeting friends," I say. "That's fine," you say, "I'll change and just tag along." Again, my old faithful companion is there, constantly ready to peer its ugly head. Tell him no. Why does he want to go with you now? Why would you want his leftover time, my mind races? I brace myself to practice grace—an unfamiliar practice for me. You quickly show up, open my car side door, as you always did, and tenderly guide me in. Suddenly, I recall that opening my side door has never stopped, not even in the worst of times.

Pride is prepared to push you away from the embrace you hold my body in as I enjoy the music. Pride is familiar, pride is faithfully present, and pride demands an answer. Why now? Why now?! I agree with pride this time and let myself lose from your embrace. I need space. I need time. I walk away with the excuse of finding a lady's room. You quickly follow and hold my hand as we walk through the crowd, dodging drinks and people moving about. Your hand tighter around mine.

Pride saying, let it go, let him go, he wanted freedom, he wanted her–remember? Now is the time to strike a blow. He wants back in, pride loudly rings, strike woman, strike! Injure him now; now is the time!

I decide to pay you an unannounced visit at your office, believing, after the weekend, that we are seeking reconciliation. I approach, and I detect the softness and kindness of intimate talk. I storm in the door, and you abruptly end your call. Guilt on your face. Why did I allow myself to believe? Why did I let you back in? You deny it all. Like Peter to Christ, you deny her more than three times. Unbelievable! Less than a minute ago, you were expressing your lust and selfish desires disguised as love. Now, you deny her very existence. It is nothing you say. She is no one, you say. She means nothing to me, you say. Well, she means something to me. She means the end of us. I storm out, upset and disappointed in myself. Why did I allow myself to be enwrapped in those calls, and what about the joy of our date? What was the invitation for the Maxwell concert for? Why on Valentine's Day? How did I let myself be fooled into believing that our flirtatious phone calls were a way back to us?

I rush home. I pack my things. I search and find the perfect apartment. I submit the application, and now I must wait the thirty days for processing. I had been hurt, disappointed, sad, and even angry for so long that I was surprised by the relief that came over me as I typed the following email.

Dear Spider & husband,

I've known of you for a while now.

I pause and remember all that I read and had educated myself about relating to affairs. They tend to last two years. Sometimes longer, if the people involved don't see each other often, daily or weekly. They often happen to men around the age of fifty. Especially when their own father has died within the two-year span of them turning or being fifty, it is their effort to not come to grips with their own mortality as they become aware that they are aging. Well, this is where I get off. I had been seeking fervently a passage in the good book that released me from the commitment I made to Christ.

I found it on this very day; *Psalms 34:14: ...seek peace and pursue it.*

Spider, this is our address. I will be moving my things out in thirty days; you are free to move in on day thirty-one. He, I am sure will be delighted to have you and welcome you with open arms.

Spider and husband, from the many emails I've read, the trips, and exchanges between both of you, I can tell that you are meant for each other. If this is love, who am I to stand in the way of love?

I wish you no harm. It will take me time to forgive. My prayer for you both is the vengeance from the Lord.

Wife

I was free, not pain-free, and not free from the sorrow or loss, but free to dream new dreams. I imagined myself in that apartment, decorating it to my own taste and my own choices. I delighted in the opportunity to read as I pleased and when I pleased. It was small, modern, and mine for a year. I started shopping for little knick-knacks. I visited my friend in the hospital often in those thirty days. Ironic, our friendship started at the start of my marriage and grew stronger with the birth of our first daughters. Now, as my marriage ended, so did her life.

I will restore you to health and heal your wounds,
declares the Lord.
Jeremiah 30:17

11

In his own words

It is a miraculous beginning to an incredible love story—a culture clash, a power struggle, a fight for independence, and ultimately a fight for control. These were just some of the challenges that stood before us, unseen but present and formidable. We were totally unprepared and only knew what we had seen—relationships that did not last and marriages that were not healthy. Our love for each other was overwhelming, and it overshadowed any concerns and responsibilities that lingered in the back of our minds, but at that same point, we would be forced to confront them because they all came crashing to the forefront. Our love story is about two incredible people from two totally different worlds who built a life for themselves and their children from sheer determination and the love we cultivated in our home. The determination to not fail to not give up lead to our healing and helped us find a better version of ourselves. The morning I received the email, I had to confront the mess I made, how far I'd come and how tired I was of living this less than genuine life.

I thought I wanted out. I knew I was seeking something easier, something new, something refreshing.

I questioned if any of this was real, ever. Had I ever loved you? Yes. Yes, I remember the promising love. I remember not wanting to be away from you. You seemed fragile but strong. Independent, but lacking worldly experience. Tender but sure of who you were and what you wanted. I had never met anyone that knew themselves and what they wanted like you did. I was taken by your beauty and your confidence. You did not require me to dim my light in any way. You were happy to sit on the sidelines and watch me fly. You were confident in the shadow of my popularity. I was eager, like a schoolboy, to fold you into my world.

Sometime during our courtship, you disclosed to me the harm your father had inflicted on you as a child. I thought you told me to be open with me, so that I could decide if to continue in the relationship or end it. I thought I registered disappointment, but that was quickly dissipated as you went on to explain that you were fine. You left that behind and had moved on. I witnessed your resilience and determination to live independently. I was happy to see you were not scarred by that experience. As our marriage unraveled, I thought it was your lack of respect for me and your inability to trust me that was hurting us. After all, I was not a perfect man, and I had caused you hurt and disappointment. I thought I could do nothing to be redeemed in your eyes. In the many trips away and abroad, I started to feel relieved to be away from you and to not have to see the disappointment in your eyes. You did not seem to value me, no matter how much I loved you or what I did to be redeemed or prove my love for you and for our family. You started to remind me of my mother in that way; in a way that I never wanted to experience again in my life. I played ball and excelled in my education and my social life. I excelled in sports as a young man. I graduated from school and went on to college on a partial scholarship and then worked to pay my way. My parents could not be part of my accomplishments. They were not present to celebrate my talents or wins in life or on the court. I had always provided the excuse, even though they never said I grew to understand the price of being a single parent like my mother and an absent parent like my father. My mother had to choose between survival and being present and engaged. She chose survival. I was grateful. My father had long ago left the family behind and moved away. I knew of him; once he returned to the city, he had left us behind. I witnessed the few exchanges between my mother and father, and they were bitter, angry, and even resentful. Sometimes, our relationship reminded me of theirs in that way. In their absence, I engaged in activities that most young men do when left to exercise their own discretion. Still, I was a good enough athlete and a good enough student to receive a partial scholarship to college. The reality and the weight of the expense of college soon set in, and I realized I could not physically or financially maintain college life.

My mother was busy working to provide for my younger sister, who was still at home, and my older sister who enrolled as a student at another college. I understood she was doing the best she could and accepted there would be no financial support, and I returned home. Soon after, with more time on my hands, in between driving my younger sister back and forth and working, my life started to get out of control. I was no longer healthy enough for myself, much less a relationship. Determined not to be another casualty of this city and this life, I moved away.

In another country, thousands of miles away, I found fame and a legion of fans admiring my talents on the court and off the court. Even then, I found myself in trouble and was at the end of serving my community service when I saw you. I, unfortunately, could not get to you at that moment, but I searched. Once I gave up my search, I found you. You ran past me, and I gave chase, setting a time to meet. I was intrigued. It was a whirlwind romance between us; even though I kept dating other women and you were in a relationship, I remember I could not wait for us to be together. We did just that. Our differences did not matter then. The culture, the religion, our customs, and the way we were raised were all things we could overcome. I was so self-assured and certain then. Even though I had never seriously considered marriage. Before I met you, I thought I would be single all my life. After we met, all that changed, and all I looked forward to, was being by your side and having you next to me.

You were scheduled for an outpatient procedure that would require transport of an hour and a half each way. You needed to be taken care of for the next few days following the procedure. I saw you soft and tender then, and I enjoyed taking care of you and your needs. Then and there is when I knew I was in love. We were in love. There was nothing that, together, we could not overcome. Our passionate embraces were no longer enough. I wanted you in my life and did not want to imagine my life without you. Our relationship was exhilarating, and your ways seductive.

I remember when I learned that you would go for walks late at night. You explained it was your time away from roommates and everyone. You enjoyed your walks alone, but I made you promise not to walk alone in the middle of the night. You reluctantly agreed. I waited around the corner from your building, late into the night, several nights - I waited. Like a stalker, I waited, but I did not care what it looked like. Nothing I did lately was making sense to anyone, including me, but I did not care. I wanted you safe, and that is how I justified my behavior. Then, there you were, walking out the door. I waited and followed quietly behind and at a distance. I wanted to be sure that you were out for a late-night walk and nothing else. Once I knew that that was what it was,

I called after you. You turned around, surprise in your eyes. I could not readily tell if you were upset because I scared you or because I might have seemed to be stalking you. As I think back on it, I readily admit that this was one of the most shameless moves I've ever made. Like I said, you were not worldly, and I thought you needed protection, and I had designated myself your protector, no matter what it appeared like at the moment. That is when I knew I was acting irrationally and isn't that what love is?

Unexpectedly, I witnessed when you ended the relationship you were in. He was walking away as I was walking to you. You informed me that you had just ended the relationship. As if I could not tell from the dejected walk of that man. I almost felt bad for him, but I was happy for what I thought meant the beginning of us. I said we would date exclusively, and I was ready to stop dating other women. It did not happen. I did all that I could to prevent you from knowing what I was doing or who else I was dating. I continued my nightlife, my dating, and my traveling, confident you were waiting for me when I returned. I enjoyed knowing you would be there when I returned. I also enjoyed my social life and was not ready to give it up. Until the day you were ready to have a social life of your own, which did not include me. I started to notice the signs that you were creating a social life of your own and enjoying new friends. All of this without me, but you still managed to always be there for me. The day you said you would not be waiting for me anymore is the day that I started taking stock of my life, and I started keeping the promise I had made to you earlier. The more we were around each other, the more certain I was that you were the one for me. I could not believe I was seriously considering being with someone for the rest of my life.

I was surprised when you rejected my offer for us to move in together. I was more surprised to hear myself ask you to marry me. I was even more surprised to find myself elated to hear you say, "Yes". Once engaged, I set about making it happen. I saw the signs and read your personal journal and your attempts to quickly move on when we had disagreements. None of that mattered to me. We were to be married. We talked about all the possible challenges and thought we were as prepared as we could be. I committed to practicing your faith, which seemed to be very important to you. Faith was not a priority in my life, and I saw no need to disagree. I even committed to having the children that we did not yet have to practice your faith. You insisted you would keep your last name, and that was the one thing I disagreed with. You would change your name and take on my last name. Full of promise and possible challenges resolved and talked through; we moved forward with our marriage plans.

The day we married, I was a proud and happy groom, and you were the most nervous and beautiful bride. We walked arm-in-arm, but I noticed that you looked pale, with sweat on your forehead, and almost about to faint; I asked, "Are you alright?" This is supposed to be the happiest day of your life, and here you were, looking beautiful but faint. Years later, I thought I should not have married you. Two years into our marriage, you said, "Okay, I have my daughter, you are now free to leave". I thought you were crazy at that time, and I stayed. We stayed, and we made our life work, in spite of and despite the obvious differences. We thought we had prepared ourselves for our differences. The ones that present themselves as challenges that would bring an end to the hope and promise we had started with. We pushed to overcome, and we did manage to navigate our differences. Compromises were central to turning you and me into us.

We lived our early years establishing a home and a family far away from the city and town that birthed us. Our community of friends grew, and with it, our social life with married friends. You met your friend Lavandi early in our marriage. She and her husband became our friends, allies, and part of our early village. Our family of three would travel for my ball games, and you cheered me on. There, in that beautiful landscape, at the bottom of a mountain, with a steady creak flowing past our backyard, we started to form us. The couple and the family we would be.

In our seventh year of marriage, I started to doubt if we would survive. I started to question if married life was for me. We were back in the United States, but you and our two daughters established a home six hours from my job. I came home on the weekends. As time went, our home together became more of a place I visited on the weekends, and my home and my life were where my job was. The geographic distance between us, over time, started to create a separation in our hearts. The weekend drives to visit you and the girls started to become a burden. My life away from the family was easier, enjoyable, and relaxing. Away from responsibility, I started to enjoy the life of a single man. The geographic and emotional distance provided all that I needed to feed my desire to be free. My career then took me even further from you and our family. I was moved from a six-hour drive to twenty-four hours away and soon after to almost 7,000 miles away. In that distance, I found the freedom I craved and had already been enjoying as a single man. All that I needed was to notify you. I was not ready for your news. "We're pregnant." I was taken by surprise, and I could tell in your voice that you were too. I had to reconsider my announcement. The timing was wrong, but I was still determined to pursue my freedom. The next time we talked, I asked you for a divorce and told you to end the pregnancy. You, yet again, managed to surprise me with your response, "we can get divorced, but I will not end the pregnancy. I can manage this pregnancy by myself. You do as you need to do." I was speechless. The determination and conviction in your voice informed me that you would not be convinced or swayed. There was no anger or disappointment that I could detect in your voice. You gave me the freedom I was seeking with no argument, no guilt trip, and no emotion. I would have what I wanted, and you would deal with the responsibility of the pregnancy and raising the family we had created. You always wanted daughters, and now you would have them to yourself, just as you had always hoped. During the pregnancy, I checked on you periodically. You experienced morning sickness at least as bad or worse than with the first two pregnancies. You were managing the demands of your career, your extended family, the pregnancy, and raising our girls, fine without me. I continued my life of a single man, enjoying all that freedom brought. The more freedom I enjoyed, the more intrigued I was with you and your determination to carry this pregnancy. Our only disagreements were about our finances and how to manage them while we were in the process of separation. It had always been easier when we were separated geographically because we knew we had always planned a way to merge them back together. This time it was more complicated. I was selfish at the time, focused on freedom and the cost of it, emotionally and financially.

No matter how far my career took me, it was routine for us to talk every day and, most days, twice a day. It was essential for us to stay connected and share about our days, with the many extended geographic separations. Now, we would talk daily, but it was no longer to build connection. I was moving on, and you were moving on. It was what I wanted, and you seemed to want it for me. As time went on, I missed our connection. My thoughts were taken by your courage and determination. I had shared with you, as a way of manipulation and my truth that I would not stay simply because you were seeing this pregnancy through delivery. You were unwavering. "I understand", you said, "I'm not asking you to." The busier I got with my outings, my social life, and my basketball, the more I started to miss our family life. I had been gone so long. I had been running from it as if it was suffocating me. I had even grown to resent the life of a married man that I had lost my way. I started to wonder if I could find a way back to this life.

Your C-section delivery was scheduled for early morning your time, and late evening my time. My friends were gathered around me as I anxiously waited on the phone for the delivery. I had suggested my name for our baby. It did not matter if our infant was born a boy or a girl. "It's a girl!" someone announced into the phone. My friends and I celebrated. I could not wait to meet her. I was anxious to get back home. I didn't know if we could repair it. I was not sure if I could find my way back, but I knew I wanted to try.

When I returned from my one-year trip, our daughter was three months old. She was more beautiful than her pictures. I questioned myself and who I was. Why would I want to walk away from our children? This family? You were not angry, but you were as resolute now as you were about the pregnancy. "The girls and I will not be joining you to where you are moving next." This time I would be nine hours away. I would not be able to come home every weekend. I wanted to raise my children myself. I wanted to give us another try. You were busy living your life. You had friends and a social life. You were busy with the girls and their activities, and being the present and intentional mom, you had always been with them. I was reminded of whom I had met years ago. Always knowing who you were and what you wanted. Resolute. At this moment, watching you thrive, I too, knew what I wanted. Once again, I would not take no for an answer. I scheduled the movers, and they came and packed our household while you were at work. I understood why you did not trust me, and I was determined to gain your trust. I just needed the opportunity. You were surprised when you returned home from work to find the movers closing the door to our household goods. "I love you, and I want our family". A month later, we were settling into our new place. We started to establish a new life together.

Everything, once again, felt new and fresh. Your career, mine, our girls enrolled in school, our live-in nanny, two cars, a great neighborhood, and new friends. Then, another trip overseas, with no set date of return. This trip was almost a year long. We talked when we could, but we were close. Our calls were light, and we laughed, and I connected with our girls. I was, once again, far in distance but close in heart. I returned to find you thriving in your career. You were busier than I was, and you enjoyed every minute of this demanding position. You were presented with an opportunity that both of us knew you could not, and as you would later share, would not refuse. It is a great opportunity you exclaimed in excitement that you could not conceal. "Imagine, NYC!" I replied with the obvious, "and our family? And the girls? Who will be here if I need to travel again?" You deserved this. I knew you deserved this more than anyone. I knew you would thrive in NYC. You had worked for this moment and had to pass up opportunities for promotions or increases because you had to stay home and raise our family while I traveled, and my career flourished. I wanted this for you, but the timing was wrong. You tried hard to work through the logistics that would make sense for our family and especially our daughters, but NYC was half-way across the country. You not only declined the position, but you resigned. You said it was best you focus your talents and efforts to help the less fortunate instead of making a fortune for companies. I don't know if that is truly why you resigned. You thrived in that environment. I think you were discouraged to accept that no matter what opportunities came your way, you still had to stand in the shadow of my career and my life. I had not valued the burdens on you or the sacrifices you made for us, for our family, and for my career. I always thought I carried the burdens of our family alone. I had to be the one that was gone. I was the one that always had a steady career and provided financial security for us. I had not noticed that my career and our family could only thrive because you were providing a steady foundation. You did what had to be done, whatever the moment called for, and I had not noticed your sacrifice until the NYC opportunity. You went on to your next position, and you thrived. Helping the less fortunate seemed to be your calling. The truth is that whatever the position and whatever the task, you would do it with more than 100% of your energy. You adapted often and easily, with no complaints, that I missed what you brought to us. I missed your gifts and talents. I missed the way you raised our daughters and your intentionality with them and with everyone around you.

Another move took me halfway across the country, and six months later you and our daughters joined me. We settled into our respective careers. We cultivated a new village for our daughters and family. We had it all and were thriving for a few years. My career once again took me back to a familiar place. The place I had sought and found freedom. The place where I was while you carried and delivered our third daughter and last child. I would be away for two years this time. Our plans for my departure were routine and solid by now. We had to prepare very little to adjust for my absence. We talked daily, but not regularly. Sometimes you could not get in touch with me because I was unavailable to you. I knew you would not be pleased with my activities. You would probably be hurt and disappointed. I noticed that sometimes I could not get in touch with you, and that was new for me. Our daughters wrote me regularly, and I exchanged letters with them. Despite our new unavailability, I was looking forward to coming home and not having to leave anymore. Two weeks before my return, you announced, "I don't think I want this anymore. I want to explore something new. I think I want a new life. I'm not in love with you anymore". I was stunned, shocked, and speechless, but I loved you, and I loved our family. I was eager to return to our life and happy to know I would not be leaving again. We sat in silence for what seemed to be a long time, but it was probably closer to a minute. I said, "Why now? As I prepare to come home". "I don't want this anymore. I don't want us. I don't know if I love you anymore." My heart was crushed because you had been my one solid foundation. "I'm coming home. I hope you are there when I get back. Give me a chance to have you fall in love with me again. If I can't get you to fall in love with me, then you can leave, but give us a chance".

We lived closer to my extended family, and I started taking regular trips there. The place that had birthed me and seen me grow up but knew nothing about my life or career and knew very little about my family. Our daughters were young ladies but adults now. The youngest one entering college. Our life in transition from young people with careers and a young family to empty-nesters, with my own father, recently passing, and still the hurt of your words in my heart. My wounds festered, and you poured salt. Your disrespect of me seemed relentless. Maybe it was, or maybe it was what it had always been, but now I was contending with my own mortality—the wound tender and in need of healing. I sought and found a reprieve that felt like healing, and I did not care enough to question what it was or where it would end. She was willing, and I was ready. You were caught up with Lavandi's illness, your brother's divorce, and your career and health in turmoil, and I was certain I wanted out. You noticed my distance and asked. I denied. You noticed my travels. You asked, and I denied. You were distracted with a new church and new friends, and I wanted nothing to do with it. Our lives growing further and further apart. The closer you seemed to get with your new church family, the more distance I created between us. I was angry and I lashed out. I denied you my affection and resented you for yours. I could not find peace, no matter where I went, how far I went, or who I was with. I felt trapped. I tried to hide. I tried to run. I tried to ignore, to no avail.

I noticed your transformation. I questioned if it was real. I wondered and resented you for the change. You were tested in your newfound faith, but you seemed to persevere. You started to serve me coffee in bed. I took notice but rejected your kindness. Your tenderness reminded me of where we started more than twenty years ago. Was this real? Was this change true and permanent? I was enraged by it all. I was restless. Uncomfortable with who I was and where I was at this moment in my life. I thought I wanted out of here, but I also wanted out of the lies and deception. I tested you. I poked at you. I rejected you. I resented you. Then came the day, the day my sister disrespected you in your home. I knew you were capable. I knew what that mouth could do. I knew you were being hit by life from many directions, but in this moment, in your home, under attack by the words of my sister, you resisted. You remained calm. I saw you extend grace. I felt shame. I felt regret. I had lost control of myself, my home, and my position in our family. You withstood and stood resolved in your faith. You lost your best friend and someone you considered your sister and confidant, and yet you stood. I saw your tears flow in that Target that Sunday morning. I had hoped to reach you but could not or did not have the courage to, and yet you stood. You moved, as you had done early in our relationship, making new friends and engaging in new activities without me. My spirit became restless. The Lord chased me wherever I went.

Your phone calls were surprising, refreshing, flirtatious, exhilarating, and new. I remembered us. I remembered you. I was tired of the disrespect, but I loved you. I had always loved you. I asked you on a date, and that evening hand in hand, I knew I wanted us. But could we find a way back to us? After our date, you had overheard one phone call too many and prepared yourself to be the one to move out.

It seemed I came to my own awakening and understanding much too late. I had never considered or connected your childhood hurts to the fights you were having with me and with yourself. I understood now. I saw the pain, and I saw the healing that was needed, but much too late now.

The mouth of an adulterous woman is a deep pit; a man who is under the Lord's wrath falls into it.
Proverbs 22:14

12

Reheated

We stayed home those thirty days. We grew solemn but gentle. We always appeared deep in thought. We not only started talking, but we started listening. We had some of our deepest and most vulnerable conversations then. We were both exhausted from the mess we had made and, in our surrender, shared our fears, hurts, and hopes freely. You allowed me to hear your heart. A heart clearly injured. You did not try to justify your behavior or explain your iniquities. Just the depth of your pain. The love that I, with my sharp tongue, turned into rage. The man whose love I turned into waste, with my constant disrespect, not realizing it was nothing more than fear—a fear protecting itself from hurt and disappointment. Your words did not seek a journey back to us; they sought only understanding.

We asked questions—questions born from pain. I know I do not deserve your respect now, and so I bare the disrespect, but the weight of the cursing and disregard, why that when I loved you so much? You continued. Even when I was preparing to return home from a long trip, I was eager to return to my family. "Do you remember what you said to me?" you asked. "What?" I ask. You continued, "You told me it was over between us, and you wanted to explore a different life. I held you in such high regard and knew I could always depend on you being there for me. You were not only my wife but my partner, the one I could always count on to always be there for me. Your words injured me deeply and damaged the way I saw you. I don't think I ever recovered from that." I hear the pain in your voice and say, "I'm deeply sorry about that." You go on with words, but you go back in your memory and ask, "Do you remember my response?" you ask me. "I asked you to wait for me and not to make that decision in my absence. I begged you to give me a chance to win you back, and if I could not get us back, then you could decide then. Do you remember?" You describe the cost of swallowing your pride to give us a chance. That evening you ended our conversation with these words, "I've always loved you. I have not been a perfect man, but even when I was not the man you needed me to be, I loved you. I just didn't understand the disrespect when I loved you so much".

Going down this lane brought healing to my hurts and cries for help. I had prayed for the Lord to reveal me to me. Suddenly, I could see me through your heart. I had occupied myself with building a fortress reinforced by pride and impenetrable, fooling myself into believing that it was strength. I had worn these words as a badge of honor that a young man bestowed upon me; "You are the manliest woman I know." He was right in his words, but I was wrong in my actions. I just could not see it then.

I saw myself as knowledgeable in all ways and thought you were lucky to partake in my wisdom. I was right always, but could not see that that made you wrong, always. I could not see that I was winning the argument but losing the fight. I was relentless with my cheap thrills that fed my ego every time I got one up on you. Everyone around me was lucky that I carried the world on my shoulders, especially you.

Night after night, we talked of the things we regretted and the things we could have done differently. Some nights we played games about our favorite things. I realized the close attention you paid to me. You knew my favorite color, my favorite vacation spot, my favorite movie, and my favorite hobby. You knew me. After more than twenty years together, I did not have answers. Even as I write these words, I'm too prideful to admit my shame that I did not know you. I had been so full of myself that I had not left room for you, to be seen or valued.

I was strong when I had to be strong, and to me, that was always. I provided homes for the homeless and comfort for the destitute. I guided and ushered the lost. I encouraged the hopeless and fed the hungry. I cared for the ill. I forgave my father and mother and provided for their care. I took in your family and mine. I cared for children and took in our friends. I was organized. I kept it moving and made it happen for the long stretches when you were gone on trips for work or for pleasure. I paid close attention to not have my pride wounded or my voice muted. I stood strong. Never again would a man take dominion over me. Never would I tolerate being struck, hit, or demeaned like my mother. Never demure, never soft, never needy. I was blinded not by my light, as my pride had convinced me of; I was lost in darkness. I had left my hometown, but I was stuck in that room, protecting that little girl.

We were the first generation in our families not to know lack. I was disciplined with money, and you trusted me with all our earnings. We owned a home and two new and always dependable luxury cars. We sent our mothers' money monthly. Raised our daughters comfortably and were in a position to help others as needed. We, like many in America, focused on building a life of comfort. We, like many in America, excused our behavior because of our good deeds for others. We, like many, got caught up in caring for many others but not ourselves. We grinded. We pushed. We achieved. We earned, and we gained, and at the same exact time, we lost—us.

As I focused on you and your perceived failures, I prayed that you would be a better husband. I punished you when you did not meet my expectations. In my perfection, I was blind. Now that I worked hard to lose you, I see you. There is no question that you are the perfect description and picture of a tall, dark, and handsome man. Why am I discovering this now? The scales of pride removed, I notice the beauty and patience of your heart. The confidence and grace by which you move. Now I value the security I found in your hands and embrace. Your commitment to always walk me to my car door to open it for me, in every season of our marriage and in all types of weather. The daily calls to me and to our daughters to check in, no matter where the job took you or for how long. Even on your trips for pleasure, the twice-daily calls did not stop. Were your eyes always this color? Were your hands always this strong? Was your love always so deep? How did you muster so much confidence and humility at the same time?

I continued to serve you coffee over days, weeks, and months, disappointed, hurt, and angry; in every season, I served you coffee. With each cup, less grumbling, less complaining to the Lord. Less, I do it out of reverence for Christ. The coffee was hotter and sweeter now that I could climb up the sixteen stairs without kicking and grumbling, a pep in my step even. I found myself trying to beat the time that you would normally get out of bed, 6:30 a.m. I'd brew it at 6:00 a.m. and pour it at 6:15 a.m. Light and sweet, I remember you telling the lady at a drive-through coffee shop. I learned to serve it light and sweet. I asked, "Tell me, do you like it like that? I do want to learn how to make it, just the way you like it." "It's perfect!" you'd say. The man you are, you would have been grateful even if it was not perfect.

We had always enjoyed our jogs together, mostly in the mornings, but sometimes in the evenings, but always together. As my sciatica had gotten worse, and your trips to the web took you away, I had missed our jogs together. Now, you invited me for walks to accommodate my joining you. I noticed now these little things that plant seeds in the soil where there once was a hard drought. You give up your routine to accommodate having my company.

We each had nothing to lose now. I had set no expectations, and you could not disappoint me. You made time to engage me and savor our time together as the time drew near for me to move out. Knowing that it was the beginning of the end gave us the freedom to be our most authentic and vulnerable selves, and we were enjoying it. We were enjoying each other.

In our marriage, you knew the things I did not like, and you made sure I did not do any of the things I did not like. I loathed getting gas. In my mind, it was a waste of time, standing there when I could be doing something else with my time, anything else. I recognize now how you continued to fill up my tank any and every time I returned from a trip, prepared to go on a trip, or returned from work. How did I think my gas tank got full every time? Of course, it had to be you. What is wrong with me? How did I not see it? In marriage, we take these routine things for granted and only grow to appreciate them once the partner is absent. I was so focused on where you were failing that I failed to notice all you did to help me thrive.

In every stage and season of our lives, droughts, floods, coffee served cold, hot, and everywhere in between, you always took the time to walk me to my car side door to open it for me, if we were going somewhere together, or if I was driving somewhere alone. Yes, even when you weren't joining me, you came outside to open my door, checked tires, washed the car, and made sure I would have all I needed so that I would not be inconvenienced in any way.

You and I never took the time to buy gifts for each other for birthdays, anniversaries, or special holidays. Our entity was always looking outwardly; we forgot to look inwardly. We also understood that we did not need gifts to express affection. If I needed something, the Lord always provided; if I wanted something, you made sure I could have it at that moment. You denied me nothing, but I also made sure not to want anything we could not afford. If you wanted something, I did not need to wait for a special occasion for you to have it. Your taste was always refined and sometimes expensive, and sometimes it would take me longer to get you what I wanted you to have, but it was not informed by a special occasion.

Music was always central in our home. You and the girls were always silly and playful. The little but everyday things that bond a family together. The girls, now grown; this would have been our time. Just you and I, back to the beginning, back to where we started, just a bit more seasoned.

Now that we had nothing left to lose, your curiosity about my Sunday morning and Wednesday and Friday evening escapes grew. You joined me to that church where you said you never would. The words you had said to me, "you will never change", you tested my commitment, and you tested it often. You questioned the softness of my ways and the authenticity of the transformation, and I did, too, more often than you.

I started looking forward to having you come home so that I could serve you a cold beer. My heart skipped a beat when I saw you relax in your man cave. Your routine, turning on the television, catching up on sports, and catching your breath. You looked so handsome and relaxed, a little grayer, but refined, sitting there with the remote in hand, a king in his castle, I thought, just like it should have always been. Happy for you that this could finally be, and happy for me that I got to witness it. A hard lesson I thought, but better late than never. We could depart as friends.

Our youngest daughter now off to college. You insist that I should keep the house. "It should be me that leaves the house, not you. You shouldn't have to leave. I messed up; I'll leave", you said. I decline. Again gracious, I thought, yes, you messed up, but I did too; you are just choosing to forget that part. You are choosing to extend me grace, plus this house with me in it, but not you is nothing more than a painful reminder of our failures. It is a shelter from a storm, but not from drought or flood. "No, I don't want it," I say. "If you can just help me move my things this weekend, I would be most grateful," you agree, and we wait for the weekend.

As the end of us draws near, we grow more protective of our time. We take fewer calls and less interruptions. Our entity investing less in others and more in ourselves. We even go on what can officially be called dates. We reviewed all that was good, all we've built together, and all that was wonderful about us, especially our daughters. We agree that is the best thing we created together. Now we try to fit in as much time for us as possible. We cook together, eat together, and share meals together. The only friends we leave time for are our new friends. The one that started out as a stranger and her husband have grown to be our confidants and guides. They stuck with us through the ugly season with patience, love, and care; no judgment, no pity, no self-righteousness, just love. The hard kind, the one nobody likes to hear, Esther, she said. Proverbs 31, remember? It's hard, I would say, but now this is harder.

The Lord, in his mercy answered my prayers and revealed me to me. As I sought your heart, I found mine.

The weekend of my move arrived. You say, "stay; this is your home. Let's take a chance, let's give us one more try. If it does not work, I will be the one to move out". We know the worst of each other, and we know our fears, our traumas, our triggers, and pain points. My pride still alive, but less pronounced, less in the leadership and protective position, and a little less present, reminds me of my words and the commitment I made to myself. "I will give you, us, all I have for as long as I'm here because I know me, and once it's over, there is no coming back." At the same time, the good word, *"let the unbeliever leave" (1 Corinthians 7:15)*. How do I go back on the word I gave to myself, that once I'm done, I'm done? How do I pass up on this beautiful apartment? My pride revisits the day, around the fire pit we had built together, the day you shared the news with our daughters that you were no longer in love with me and would be moving out. That was shortly after our 2-hour talk.

Can we recover from all the pain, hurt, and disappointments we've caused each other? Can we truly forgive? Not forget. I knew I would not forget, but is forgiveness possible and enough?

Is this the drought or the flood? In a drought, isn't it better to pack up and plant seeds somewhere else? If you stay, how do you know if the dry land will ever produce anything healthy again? Is there life beneath this dry land? If this is a flood, is there enough foundation left to rebuild, scrub off all the dirt and grime, and get to the studs? Either a flood or drought, the task after a devastating event, is monumental. Are we up for this work? Are we up to the task of building something that we ourselves destroyed?

We begin the painstaking work, one pile of trash at a time. After each heavy lift, we find something we treasure. We also found painful reminders that challenged our resolve. We set two ground rules on this road to recovery: love and respect. Not that one of us would demand respect and the other would demand love, but that when we felt disrespected or unloved, we would call each other higher. We would not challenge it or question it; we would just believe what the other was experiencing based on our actions. Our response to calling each other higher would be the measure of our progress and sincere efforts to recovery.

We took the time to focus on ourselves. This was not an agreement or a rule, but this happened organically, as a result of wanting a better us as a result of enjoying each other's company more. As a result of God's lover, mercy, and grace. In these moments together, we talked about our dreams and plans for the future. We committed ourselves to prayer and studying the good book, sometimes together and sometimes alone. The closer we drew to each other and to God, the more critics came. They were swift and varied. We received criticism and skepticism from family and friends. Criticism for taking steps back and away from them, our extended family. We held our ground and protected our time, each other, and our interests. People challenged the transformation of our lives together; they would bring up our past, and they would test if we knew each other's secrets, threatening our resolve and commitment to each other. If you don't give way or give in, some friends and some family will be happy and celebrate your commitment, and others will fall away. Our new journey was uncomfortable for them. We held on to God, we held on to each other, and we stayed the course. We remained silent, letting our walking do the talking. Control being a way that I fed my fears, I practiced giving up control and handed the budget over to you. You rose to the occasion, and you were more thoughtful and disciplined about our giving to others but prioritized us. We set a budget for our dates and our own expenses or allowance for each other. We also set a budget for our parents that was more predictable and therefore manageable and prioritizing us over family. Over time I realized just how much relief this provided for me. Giving up control made me feel cared for, and our allowances to each other were a gift that required more discipline and thoughtful spending on my part. The arguments about spending came to a complete halt. Giving it over was transformative for me in that it starved my need for control. Eventually, I realized my fears subsided, and I grew to trust you and trust God for my provision. I enjoyed your leadership and practice. You became 2nd in my life, only after God, as the good book calls for. This included me gathering our daughters and apologizing to them for my years of disrespect to you, the bad example I was for them as a disrespectful wife, and my need for control. I confessed to them that my need for control and living in strength was nothing more than fear of living in vulnerability. I shared where my fear came from and that this was part of my healing process. Moving forward, I would be submitting to your leadership, and I had been wrong in my stronghold of the house. They all protested and decried this change, but inside I think they were giddy and happy for my healing journey but still had their doubts that I would submit. Me too, but it was a journey, and I invited them to hold me accountable. They did just that, saying, "is that what it says in the bible, mom?" I'd roll my eyes, and we'd laugh.

Change is hard on everyone, but once we obeyed and practiced, we found that we enjoyed each other's companionship more and more. His reward for our obedience. We set the budget, always including enough for our dates. Once the date arrived, it made it easier to have fun; no pressure about how much to spend and how it would impact our budget or others that might call for urgent help. This was our commitment to place each other first and God in the center. We continued to call each other during our workdays; we were committed to keeping it brief so that we could be flirtatious with each other and not give into the temptation to begin to get distracted and talk about family, friends, bills, chores, just flirting, sometimes silly and sometimes steamy, but always good for our soul. We talked about responsibilities, chores, and those things that are less fun, once a week if needed, but at least 1 to 2 hours monthly for planning purposes and to be able to keep the light of our connection all the other days of the week. We used to take turns cooking before, but it was based on who got home from work first. Now we made it a point to cook together a few days out of the week, and since music was always a part of our home, these cooking times would lead to unexpected dancing. Sometimes just the two of us and sometimes with family present. It always made our evenings fun and playful: the bad singing, the good dancing, and the great food.

We made it a point to find time to get away together. Although we were occasionally empty nesters, we would still make it a point to get away from home and responsibilities together. The first time we did, it had been so long since we had been alone for fun, just the two of us, that it was a fantastical disaster. I will spare the details because it was not cute, but it was hilarious to us. We were not deterred, and we tried again and again and again. The more we practiced, the better we became at it. We started to enjoy our stolen moments with each other. You challenged me in the intimacy department just to kiss a little longer than a peck and then in public. Only when challenged did I realize just how much I enjoyed the challenge. I still don't feel fully comfortable expressing affection in public, but occasionally I surprise you and initiate these moments of affection because I see that they bring you joy, and that makes me happy, and it draws us closer together. Now our girls find it disturbing that my ringtone when you call is *Sexual Healing* by Marvin Gaye.

Your trips home happen less often, but even when they happen, you make sure to invite me. Sometimes, I join you, and sometimes I don't, just to provide you space and time with your mother and siblings. Many may wonder, do I trust you? How do I trust you? Do I doubt? Am I fearful? You have taken it upon yourself to make me comfortable in every way. You call me often; you call me in the middle of the night. Although I say this is not necessary, you always respond with, "I want to. I want you to be the last person I talk to before I fall to sleep. I want you to know where I am. I want to be sure you know you can call me anytime if you need to". Even with extra effort, people can find ways to fall into temptation, and I know this. You and I are included in these people. So, do I trust you? I don't know. I can't say that I do or that I don't; even now I don't give this much thought. I trust God. I don't worry about you, or us, or tomorrow, or me, or any past or future her or him, because I trust God. If tomorrow you or I fall, God will be there to lift you or me up. He will see us through together, or he will see us through apart. Either way, I trust that He will be more than enough. I don't worry about tomorrow because it will rob me of enjoying us – today.

And after you have suffered a little while, the God of all grace, who has called you to his eternal glory in Christ, will himself restore, confirm, strengthen, and establish you. (1 Peter 5:10)

13

Refined

The day we married, we were young; you were seven years my senior, and we were both thousands of miles from the families we had grown up with as children. You were an eager and happy groom. I was a nervous but trusting bride. It was a small ceremony in a foreign language. Only a few close friends were invited and came to celebrate with us. On that day, far from home. God gave us a gift, we did not recognize it then, but it was a treasure that sustained us through our ego and the arrows that were to come and test us. Together we cultivated a culture of two worlds that help transform us, pain by pain, joy by joy, struggle and triumph, lessons and life, into our own values and beliefs, way before the generations before us could insert their wills, beliefs, bitterness, and experiences. The mess we made was influenced by our childhood experiences, but it was ours, and there was no one else to blame. The culture of our marriage was cemented, but no matter how far from home we were, loads of ghosts from our past experiences haunted our present—your need to be seen and my need to be heard.

The risks we take and the calculated moves we make with each move creating or destroying, and each action cultivating or killing. What is certain is that the word is living and true, but with lots of mercy—that which we sow, we reap.

I thought that when I married you, I did not love you, but I trusted your love for me. The truth that only God knew then and was only revealed to me over time, pain, healing, and triumph, is that the love I needed was trust. The trust I labeled ease on our first date, back on that 4th of July. Trust in the hand of God that guided me to take a leap of faith and say yes to your marriage proposal, despite my hurts and fears. The trust to know that all that you were was all that I needed. God, in his mercy, plucked me out of my mess from the hurts caused by the sins of my father and the ones I carried. God, in his grace, plucked you from your mess, a child that was missed and not seen, and provided you with the talents and gifts to not only be seen but to shine. And shine you did, with your thoughtfulness, with your kindness and care. You shined on the court and off the court. As your uncle said, once he saw the podcast of our daughters for you on that Father's Day, "it makes me wish you were my dad." Yes, I agree; me too. Thoughtful in the way you cared for your dad when he got sick and brought him to our home. You were tender and loving towards him, even though he left you when you were two years old. You opened not only our home, but your heart to him. Attentive in the way you cared for our daughters as adult women now. You wash and maintain their cars; you fill up their tank, one of their hearts, and their cars. You make sure they know they don't ever have to put up with any abuse or anything that minimizes them; this is always a home they can return to. You take the time to befriend all their friends so that we know them and respond accordingly. As they say, the only words we don't want to hear from dad are that he is disappointed in us. That speaks to your character and the extent to which they honor you. They have no illusion of you as a perfect man, but even your flaws are so minor in their eyes because of all that you have cultivated in them as children and as adult women. You are admired by many but honored by few, and those few are us, the ones that matter, the ones that witness you daily and see all of you, and still, we remain in awe of you. When we talk about you, we always admire that although you might have much to grumble about, you never have, not once, about anything.

The Lord is wise beyond our capacity to understand, and he knew where we started and knew what we needed, always even more than we knew ourselves. We came together like two wounded children, a city boy from Jersey and a country girl from Texas, in a foreign land at just the right time, far from our start but closer to us. He knew that in the heat, he would provide healing. The Lord knew you had the strength, stamina, and confidence, to help guide me into healing.

I can't explain today how I see all of you, know the good, see the imperfections, and yet I love you more today than yesterday. I know that tomorrow when I wake up, I'll be grateful that I'm lying next to you. I'll be up and awake early in the morning, and in my quiet time with God, I will be humbled by our journey; I will be grateful for this mess that he has carefully converted into a masterpiece. We were just the clay. I will look at you and see you, a day older but so much more handsome each day, and I will be grateful for you. Your stamina, your commitment, your love, the father you are, and the husband you have been and are to me. I will rise from bed and happily cook your breakfast, pack your lunch, and at 6:00 a.m. I will brew our favorite coffee, Black and Bold. I will pour it at 6:30 a.m., prepare it light and sweet, and as I walk up the stairs, giddy to serve you, in our bed, in our beautiful home, I will pray that it is perfect to your taste. As I walk out of our bedroom every morning, I smile in gratitude that I found love, the love that one gives without expectation, the love that brings joy, that love that is sacrificial, the one that binds and keeps no records of wrong, I found this love for you in serving you a cup of coffee.

Five young and beautiful ladies hurried, running around, lining up shoes, hanging up dresses, applying make-up, and fixing up hair. Three beautiful women about my age, sitting in chairs, almost uncomfortable with being fussed over and primped and polished. The most gorgeous woman, smiling, a picture of strength, class, and charisma, being dressed in her gown. Just then, I realize, she has no need for primping, polishes, or gowns, because her shine comes from within, and her attire is the dignity and grace by which she has lived her 101 years of life. I notice the woman whose hands are tender and caring and whose smile always exudes the love without borders that has guided her sacrificial life. A woman whose youth, poise, and beauty do not say I have raised ten children and loved thirty-four grandchildren. No bitterness or resentment can be found, not because of the abuser she married, not because of the seven children she did not know about, not for the bruises on her body that have left no signs of a scar on her heart, not even for a lifetime of servitude. No, just beauty, gratitude, joy, and love, always love. As I watch her, I pray, Lord, please let me love just a morsel of how my mother loves. I smile, and my heart skips a beat as I take in the room and realize that at this very moment in my life, the Lord has found a way to answer many prayers. Thank you, God; I see me more and more through your eyes. Thank you, Father, that I am no longer the source of my own nightmares. Thank you,

God, for Esther, the example of a woman I aspire to be. Thank you for the three women that I birthed and the two others that I did not, but all the same, they are women I would like to have as friends. Thank you, God, for my grandmother's determination and courage. Thank you, God, for my mother, who has been an example of sacrificial and unconditional love. Thank you, God, for my church family, my pastor, and his wife, an example of Christ's love and life. Thank you, God, for letting me know the joys of being a grandmother. Thank you for the "Breezes" in my life. And now, God, as I am summoned by my squad, five-deep, I thank you for the true and deep love, connection, passion, and mutual respect, between my husband and me. This journey into the next phase of our lives together.

He is the tall, dark, handsome one at the end of the aisle, with a $1,500 suit but a 1-million-dollar smile, but this time I see him, and yes, time has been kind to him because he is fine and refined, and I hear him say...

My Love for My Wife

Thirty years ago, on the other side of the sun,

We fell in love and then became one.

I remember your beautiful eyes, your lips and skin,

That gorgeous complexion of Latin descent.

We lived so careless, so selfish and so free

While living that way, we created three.

I've departed so many times to the army's song

So confident and assured that you will carry on.

The path we chose was an unpredictable life

The decisions the sacrifices of an army wife.

To watch our family, grow with blessings and grace

To be re-assured as we grow in our faith.

The lives of our girls and the path they've chosen

The love of our family that will never be broken

The life we live, is the life we make

I still want to be the first breath you take

Some chapters in our lives have come to an end

The way it looks to me is here we go again.

To share this occasion was a must

To re-new our vows in God we trust.

These words I say

I'm trying to explain

That I am so proud that you carry my name.

Husband

We watch or lives in pictures, no sign there of scars or pain, as we listen to Jeffrey Osborne sing the words to The Greatest Love Affair.

New Beginnings (The End)